PLANET WINE

Stuart Pigott

PLANET

A GRAPE BY GRAPE VISUAL GUIDE TO THE CONTEMPORARY WINE WORLD

WINE

MITCHELL BEAZLEY

PLANET WINE

by Stuart Pigott

First published in Great Britain in 2004 by
Mitchell Beazley, an imprint of Octopus Publishing
Group Limited, 2–4 Heron Quays, London E14 4JP.

A CIP catalogue record for this book is available from
the British Library.

ISBN: 1 84000 776 1

The author and publishers will be grateful for any
information that will assist them in keeping future
editions up-to-date. Although all reasonable care has
been taken in the preparation of this book, neither
the publishers, editors nor the author can accept any
liability for any consequences arising from the use
thereof, or the information contained therein.

Commissioning Editor Hilary Lumsden
Executive Art Editor Yasia Williams
Design Tim Pattinson
Managing Editor Juanne Branquinho
Editor Jamie Ambrose
Picture Research Emma O'Neill, Juanne Branquinho,
Stuart Pigott
Index Ann Parry
Production Gary Hayes

Typeset in Versailles and Vectora

Printed and bound by Toppan Printing Company
in China

The spreading wide my narrow Hands
To gather Paradise

Emily Dickinson

ACKNOWLEDGEMENTS

THANKS to all those at Mitchell Beazley and beyond
who believed that a manned mission to Planet Wine
was possible. Many helped knowingly, others did so
unknowingly and without all of them the eagle would
never have landed. A special thank you goes to
Carole Meredith of University of California, Davis and
Fedinand Regner of Klosterneuburg in Austria who
provided invaluable information from the cutting
edge of vine genetic analysis.

PLANET WINE

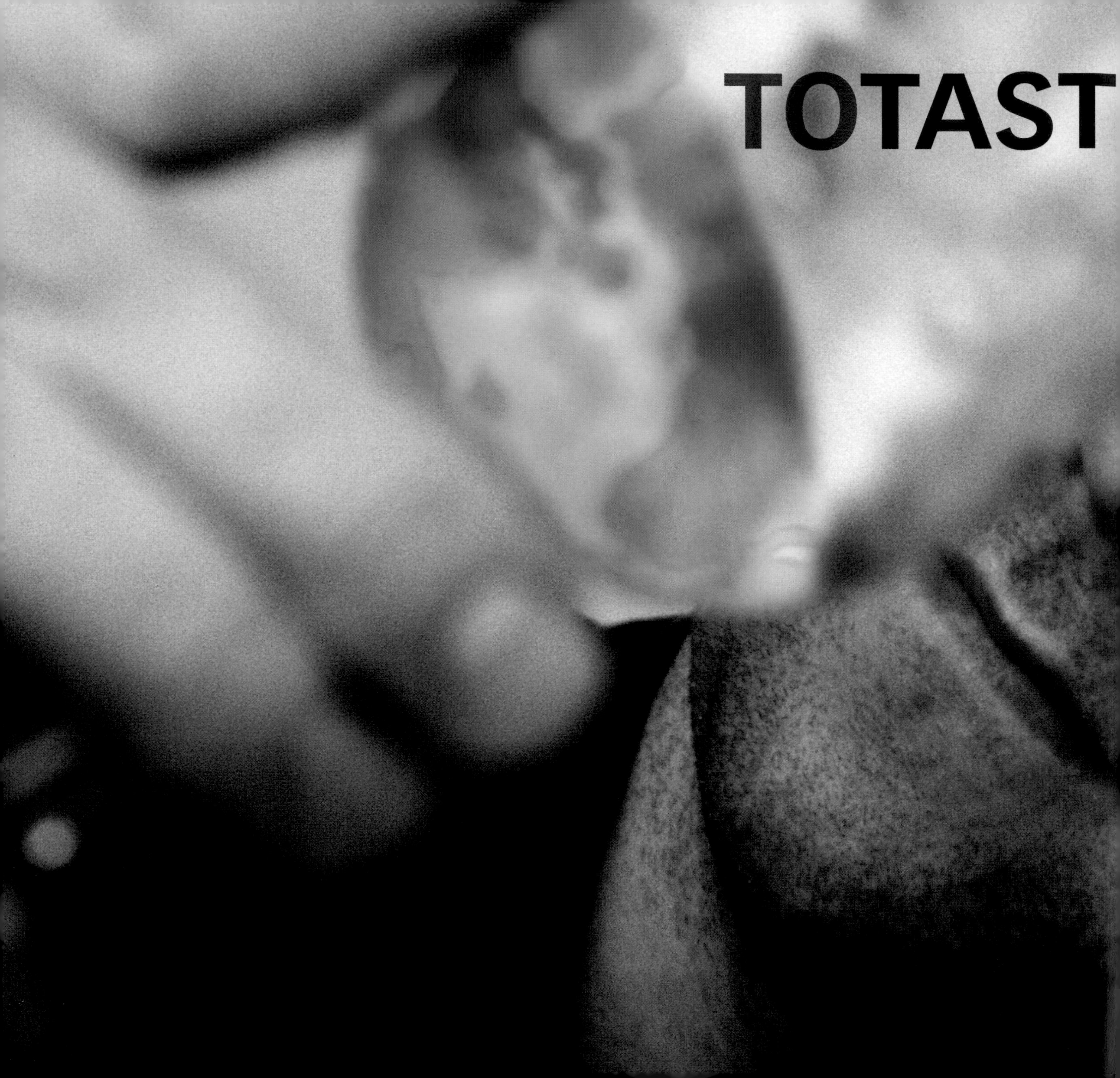
TOTAST

ETHEWORLD

Welcome to Planet Wine. Don't worry; I hear you. "How can a glass of wine contain a whole world?" Just as every picture tells a story, so every wine spins a tale of the grapes that created it, of the place it came from, and of the people who made it. If you open your mind, you *can* take a slurp of a faraway world – you already do, in fact, without being aware of what's happening in your nasal cavity, mouth, and nervous system.

"Are we all budding wine experts, then?" Well, yes. However little or much you know, the pleasure of discovery is only as far away as the next glass. The only thing most people lack is a modest amount of information to interpret what their senses tell them. It's the name of the grape variety on the label that provides the prime key to understanding wine. That's why this book has been created: to show you how to turn that key and open the door to more pleasure. So if you want to taste the world, read on.

Grape Varieties Genetic and Flavour Diversity

During the wine boom of the late-twentieth century, a large handful of grape varieties that combined good flavours with climatic adaptability were planted around the globe, turning them into something resembling global brands. At the same time, however, dozens of other grape varieties established themselves in climatic niches big enough to make them significant facets of Planet Wine. Their names might look unfamiliar at first, but they are often more difficult to pronounce than to enjoy. They are part of a global backlash against the homogenization of wine flavours which began during the 1980s.

I tasted it on
the grapevine

Chardonnay, Cabernet Sauvignon, and Shiraz have already become household names – like Granny Smith and Golden Delicious. They aren't just the names of wine types, though, but of grape varieties that taste every bit as different from one another as different apples do. This is the first thing you smell and taste in any good wine: the genetic fingerprint of the grape variety. Which wines you or I prefer has a great deal to do with the grape varieties from which they were made. Vine genetics are as varied and specific as human fingerprints. Each variety, and each clone of each variety (Planet Wine has been inhabited by clones for decades), has its own signature aromas and hallmark balance.

Not so long ago, Planet Wine wobbled on its axis when, behind the scenes, a revolution in vine genetic analysis revealed the truth about many grape varieties. We've discovered a great deal about the origins and relationships between vine varieties, and the news has often been surprising. Just as many royal families have benefited from injections of "common" blood, the same is true of many of the so-called noble grapes. Be warned: throughout this book, you'll find out the shocking truth about the ancestry of the world's favourite grapes.

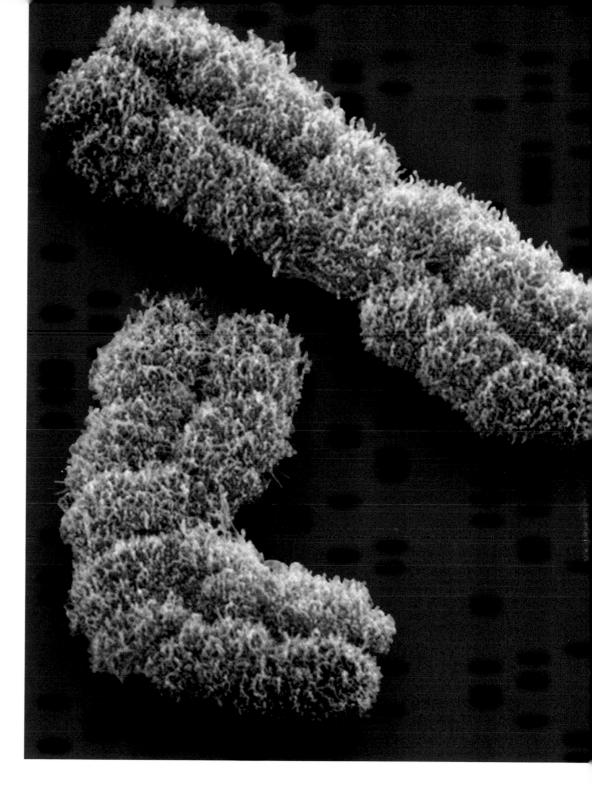

Terroir **Capturing the Taste of the Place**

Wine is not the only agricultural product whose smell and taste are influenced by where it grows. While tea, coffee, chocolate, honey, and olive oil (to mention only a few) are also similarly affected by their growing enviroments, none of them approach the precision with which certain wine grapes "record" the landscape and conditions under which they ripened, or the way that the wines made from these grapes can "replay" that world in the glass.

Today, almost every wine is clean and correct, filled with the fruity taste of the grape variety from which it was made: this is the first dimension of wine. The second and third dimensions, those things that make wine exciting, fascinating or even irresistible, are its style and origin – meaning *who* made it and *where* it came from. Any wine that is not mass-produced will have both these qualities, and a great wine has them by the bucket-load. Style is the product of the winemaker's aesthetic feeling for wine, while origin shows itself in the aromas and flavours that come from the vineyard, the specific environment in which it grew, and climatic conditions. The French have a word for this: terroir. Today it is a buzz-word all over Planet Wine.

"Wine is sunlight held together by water"

Galileo

For Gallic traditionalists, the T-word "terroir" means literally the taste of the soil, but in most places on Planet Wine, terroir is understood as the interplay of the vineyard's latitude and exposure to the sun with climatic factors and the soil. Put simply, this means that wines from the same grape variety grown in different wine regions, or even two neighbouring vineyards but treated identically in the cellar, will taste different from one another. Although professionals analyze terroir logically, something enigmatic always remains. In vineyards, no less than in the wine in your glass, natural and human factors are intertwined so intextricably that you can never untangle them completely.

Today, a great many vineyards, particularly those whose produce is destined for low-priced bottles, are cultivated entirely mechanically, the grapes untouched by human hand. The quantity produced is also important, for the production cost per unit of grape juice determines which price point the wine can hit on the shelf. It was thirty years ago that the introduction of drip irrigation and mechanical harvesters made this approach possible. Intensive cultivation by hand is the other extreme, and key to the quality of the world's most exciting wines. As different as the two approaches are, both are all about growing flavour. Whatever the final price of the wine-growing, flavour is a challenge.

Growing Flavour
From Bud-break to Juice

If you let vines do what they want, then they literally start climbing trees. The pruning and training of vines are as strict as any corset – the means of persuading the plants to stand upright and ripen grapes, instead of creating jungles. How a vineyard is planted is not only determined by the idiosyncracies of the grape variety and the climate in which it grows, but also with how the vine will be cultivated.

Let your
garden grow…

The labour-intensive method is all about the expense-is-no-object struggle to nurture every bunch to perfect ripeness. In many places on Planet Wine it is a problem to find people willing to do the work, such as this skilled Mexican labourer (*right*) in California's Napa Valley. Vineyard managers might wear old jeans and boots, but they are actually like chess players who must not only react to every move of their opponent, the weather, but also try to anticipate what its next move will be. The grape – sugars (that fermentation converts into alcohol), acids, aromas, tannins, and colour – ripen at different rates. And every growing season is different from the one before. In recent years, many vineyard managers have turned to organic or biodynamic cultivation methods (which follow lunar and cosmic cycles) in order to strengthen the vines' natural resistance to fungal disease, pests, and drought stress, rather than using chemicals to fight them. For the fundamentalists, this is also the key to ripening everything in the grape simultaneously and achieving cosmic harmony in the glass. For the pragmatists, these methods are about making a more distinctive wine with respect for the environment.

High-tech Winemaking Future Perfect?

The winemaker can ignore nature in the form of the grapes and simply impose his or her will upon them. Good winemakers reject this path in favour of working *with* nature, using the most gentle processing methods possible, to capture all that is good in the grape while excluding from the wine anything that could endanger its clarity or harmony. For them, technology is only the means to this simple end. The bad winemaker is like a compulsive egomaniac, while the good winemaker is closer to a Zen Buddhist. Take your pick.

Like the food industry, the wine industry's production methods have made gigantic "advances" during the last decades. Bad – unclean or oxidized – wine has effectively been consigned to the dustbin of history. The standardization of wine flavour has been the downside of this revolution. Serve a typical, modern, dry white wine and its red counterpart at the same temperature to a blindfolded expert, and she or he could have difficulty in deciding which is which. Full, fruity, and round became an all-too-common formula for whites and reds alike during the 1990s. But producers love the fact that the units keep moving by the million...

Another product of the high-tech factor is the irresistible allure that glittering new machinery exerts on certain winemakers: the people who were called "cellarmasters" just a generation ago. Machines such as the Must Concentrator (for fattening up any wine the winemaker deems to be anorexic by extracting water from the grape juice or wine), or the Spinning Cone (for slimming down anything deemed overweight by the winemaker by partially de-alcoholizing them), sound a bit like *Terminator*. Enzymes that promote the development of certain aromas and gene-manipulated yeasts that can shape wines even more radically are other weapons in the contemporary winemaking arsenal. Today, in some highly automated cellars, wine is virtually handmade by robots.

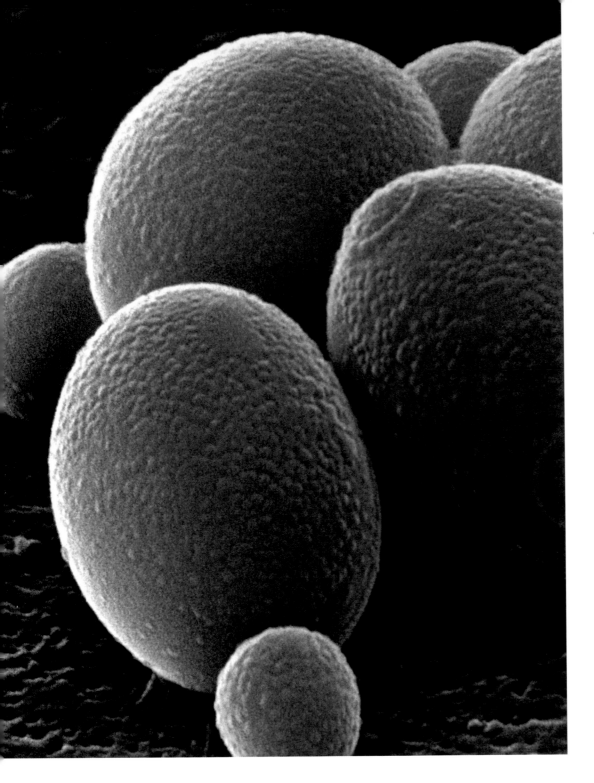

Nude and unabridged

For the same reason that the introduction of the CD lead to a resurgence of interest in valve amplifiers and vinyl, the arrival of modern winemaking technology resulted in a revival of "old-fashioned" cellar methods and equipment. Today's pioneers of "natural" winemaking prefer techniques and machinery from earlier centuries because they are gentler on the grapes and wine than the modern alternatives. Their goal is wines with the same palpable warmth and energy as music on vinyl. Old wooden barrels like these stacked in the Niepoort lodge in Vila Nova de Gaia in Portugal, which enable the wine maturing in them to breathe without getting the taste of oak, have become a symbol for this purist approach. However, the unplugged school of winemaking is not dependent upon any specific cellar technology, rather is all about playing it absolutely straight in order to capture the flavour of the grape without any distortion. To make this point winemaker Martin Tesch of the Nahe region in Germany called one of dry whites "Unplugged" to make it clear that it is the Riesling grape without amplification or remixing.

Low-tech Winemaking **Unplugged**

Wild yeast is the trump card of the low-tech school of winemaking, whose members believe (sometimes with an almost religious zeal) that, left to its own devices, nature will come up with something far more captivating than anything man can think up. A wild-yeast fermentation is unpredictible, however, because dozens of strains of yeast are involved – unlike when a single type of cultured yeast is added. The theory is that this results in complex, rather than simple aromas and flavours.

"Look, ma: no hands!" Low-tech winemaking is a risky business – like swinging from a trapeze without a net or riding a Harley Davidson without holding the handlebars. When things go wrong, the result can be lifeless and unclean wines: those "old" wine problems that have become so rare in everyday drinking wines. But when everything works, the result is a taste as immediately haunting as the sound of Nirvana or Eric Clapton unplugged…

The world's first wine fad was for red bordeaux in seventeenth century London. This was started by François-Auguste de Pontac of Château Haut-Brion when he opened The Pontac's Head, just off Newgate Street, 1666. This original "wine bar" was named after the owner's father (*left*), Arnaud de Pontac III, the estate owner who had begun exporting his wine to England a few years before. It was an instant hit with fashionable society; Samuel Pepys praised both the establishment and its wines in his diary. If it had not been for the de Pontacs' entrepreneurial spirit and the excitement of Pepys and his contemporaries, we might never have heard of Bordeaux and many of its vineyards might still be marshes.

Wine Fashions **and Marketing**

The wine industry has long been a fashion industry. This means that if anyone deliberately drinks a particular type of wine with attitude, it becomes a style statement and possibly starts a new trend. If this sounds like the fashions in clothes, hairstyles, music, and pop culture, then it is because wine has been subsumed into pop culture. The only difference is that most pop culture does not grow in fields or undergo alcoholic fermentation – which is why wine fashions move slower.

The latest mega-trend in wine circles began in November 1991, and was caused by the widely reported claims of doctors that moderate red wine consumption can help prevent heart disease. All kinds of factors can create a trend in the wine world – not least improved quality, as happened to Greek wines during the late 1990s. What is the next trend? If Greece can do it, then Thailand can, too. Bizarre as it might sound, our favourite holiday destination in southeast Asia now produces enough wine to export; the best red and white Thai wines are up to international standards, and the nation has a fundamentally positive image. All they need is a determined sales push and some clever PR, though maybe they should avoid the kind of packaging Piper-Heidseck Champagne once tried! It's one tight dress that Jean-Paul Gaultier will want to forget too...

Feel the buzz,
taste the sizzle

Here is one of the most powerful men on Planet Wine – and he knows it. Until very recently, Robert Parker (*below*), publisher and main author of *The Wine Advocate*, and Marvin Shanken, publisher of *Wine Spectator*, were jointly calling almost all the shots in the global market from their HQs on the American east coast. Determined to challenge their hegemony, a group of French wine journalists formed the *Grand Jury European*, but this joint European fleet was no match for the two carrier groups of the Americans. Wine-lovers and collectors from Tokyo to Berlin preferred the shoot-from-the-hip numerical rating of individual wines supplied by the Yanks to the more plodding approach of the Europeans.

Wine Media and Wine Collectors

Wine collecting is an increasingly common syndrome. Previously confined to older men, in recent years it has spread rapidly to younger men and women of all ages. Its prime symptom is a compulsive need to hoard wine bottles in the bottom of wardrobes, under the stairs, and in all manner of other dark, confined spaces. Sufferers show an obsession with cold, damp, subterranean rooms. Tragically, as yet, no effective treatment is available…

Shocked by Trainspotting? Just wait for the ugly sequel Winebuffing!

If you are sometimes shocked by the prices of certain wines – and the prices for sought-after wines exploded during the last decade – then one of the prime reasons for this is the influence of wine collectors and investors. A collector is anyone who puts more wine in his or her cellar than he or she drinks, while an investor is anyone who – heaven knows why – would rather resell good wine for a profit than drink it. The prices of all the cult wines, whatever their colour or type, result from the combined interests of these two types of consumer as well as the critics' ratings, which are always stoking the fires of demand.

BATTLEO

FTHE**GIANTS**

1 Here on Planet Wine, wine-growing nations, multinational corporations, and grape varieties vie for supremacy. As far as the wine in your glass is concerned, the most important player is the latter. During the last two decades, it was big wines – giants with as much body as a sumo wrestler and a Mike Tyson-style punch of flavour – that won the hearts of the media, opinion leaders, and wine buffs around the world. For many of them, wine descriptors such as "light", "delicate", and "elegant" were simply synonyms for "thin" and "characterless" – and any wine that wasn't big and brassy enough to be "in yer face" was out of place. While the grip of this prejudice upon Planet Wine has waned, the appeal of this type of wine hasn't. Why? Because when it's done right, big *can* be beautiful…

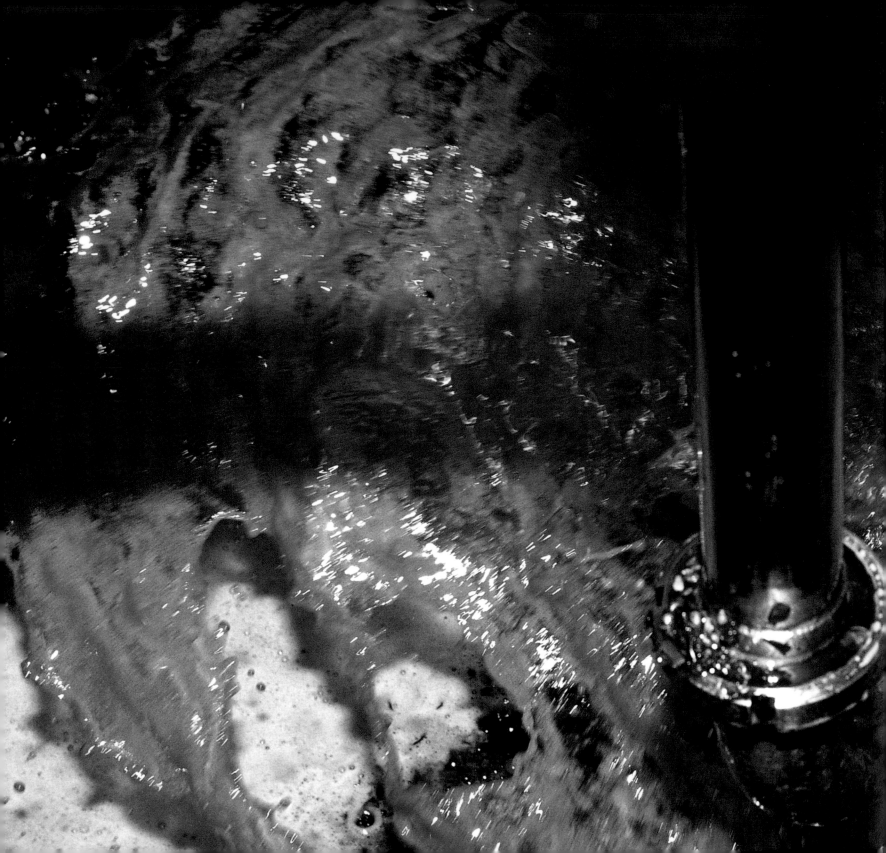

Cabernet Sauvignon

This glorious mass of black grape-skins, purple fermenting wine, and pips is how every great Cabernet Sauvignon wine begins life. The greater part of its hypnotic appeal and indisputable power come from the skins, out of which the wine extracts colours, aroma, and tannins during fermentation. The latter give the wine its backbone, strength, and texture. This process can take several weeks, during which the young wine is "pumped over" the skins, or the skins are "punched down" into the wine to accelerate the extraction rate. It's a tightrope act, because "overextraction" leads to hardness: a pile of bones with too little flesh to cover them properly. A great Cabernet is like an athlete whose skeleton is clothed with taut muscles but no unnecessary fat so that he can sail through the tape at the end of a marathon. A bad Cabernet is more like a muscle-bound weight-lifter who has trouble getting though doors and into chairs.

Welcome to the Elysian Fields of Cabernet

While the wines of many grape varieties lose their personality when grown on the flat, many of the world's greatest Cabernet Sauvignons come from vineyards with almost imperceptible slopes that look flat at first glance. This is as true of the Médoc in France as it is of Margaret River in Western Australia, the Napa Valley in California or Bolgheri in Tuscany. >>

What the Cabernet Sauvignon vine demands, then, is a free-draining soil that prevents it from getting cold, wet feet: something no vine hates more than this sun-worshipper. Given these conditions, it can turn sunlight and warmth into black skins packed with purple colour, the aromas of blackcurrants and plums, and a balance in which sumptuous richness is precisely counterpointed by noble dryness.

A mild coastal climate helps give reds from Cullen and Moss Wood in Margaret River, Araujo and Château Montelena in Napa Valley, and Ca' Marcanda and Ornellaia in Bolgheri their combination of power and refinement. In the Médoc, where sun is scanter, the vineyards located next to the Gironde Estuary benefit from extra warmth and a more expansive sky. That's what you taste in the ripe and boldly expressive wines from Ducru-Beaucaillou, Latour, Léoville-Las-Cases, Montrose, and Sociando-Mallet.

Cabernet Sauvignons from genuine mountain vineyards will always be expensive, because of high cultivation costs and small crops per vine. However, the Cabernets from vineyards in the shadow of mountains don't have to break the bank, as Chilean and Argentine wines prove. There, irrigation water from Andean snow and glaciers makes some of the best-value Cabs on Planet Wine possible. The rest of the credit must go to the winemakers who, a decade ago, mastered the art of capturing all the grape's fruit character in a supple package of tannin and alcohol. They proved that when it comes to this grape, soft-rock doesn't have to be a cop-out. >>

Though many of the best wines from the Cabernet Sauvignon grape grow on flat vineyards (*see* pages 26–7), this vine is also a daring mountaineer. It relishes nothing more than putting its roots down into rocky soil on slopes where the contour lines are so tightly packed together that cartographers tear their hair out. The obvious advantages of being up above the clouds, as at Rustenberg (*left*) on the slopes of the Simonsberg, close to Stellenbosch in South Africa, are that the day is longer and the sunlight has a greater intensity than on the plains below. The advantage you cannot see is the fresh mountain air which helps give "Mountain Cabernet" a brightness of aroma (wild berries) and a freshness that enables monster wines to effortlessly glide across your palate.

Hard rock Cabernet
vs
soft rock Cabernet

In the hands of masters, Mountain Cabernets gain a wild mix of herb and spice aromas from the rocky soil and achieve the same kind of miraculous combination of power and energy as Mohammed Ali, when the heavyweight champion of the world danced like a butterfly and stung like a bee. On the hillsides over Napa Valley, the star producers are Cain, Dalla Valle, Harlan Estate, Shafer, and Viader (*above*), while in South Africa they are Buitenverwachting, Rustenberg, de Trafford, and Vergelegen.

Which type of oak is best for barrel maturing Cabernet Sauvignon reds is a subject of endless debate among winemakers. Robert Mondavi (*left*), of the eponymous Napa Valley winery, always contended that French oak was better aged and coopered than the home grown kind, resulting in a drier and more sophisticated wine. It wasn't long after he began using French oak barrels in 1966 that most of California's leading Cabernet Sauvignon producers followed his lead. Today, many Californian wineries spend seven- or eight-figure dollar sums on French oak barrels every year. They do it because they think we like our Cabernet flavoured with 200 plus year-old oak trees. Is that what we really want, though?

Taming the beast Cabernet

Oxygen is the winemaker's equivalent of the animal tamer's whip, but it must work slowly on the wine if the process of civilization is to be completely successful. Usually, oxygen is administered through the wooden sides of barriques, oak barrels that are 228 litres in size, where the wines sojourn for twelve to thirty months. For Cabernet Sauvignon, this is the equivalent of a stay at the best Swiss finishing school. >>

Paul Draper of Ridge (*right*) contends that, today, the best American oak barrels are of the same standard as the finest French ones. He also believes that they better tame the Californian beast, yielding a more seductive wine. You decide who is right.

High above Silicon Valley, only an hour-and-a-half's drive south of San Francisco, poisonous snakes slither between the rows of Cabernet Sauvignon vines in Ridge's Monte Bello vineyards. However ripe the grapes get in great Cabernet Sauvignon vineyards like these, there's always something a little wild about the red wines that come from them – especially when they're young. Tasted from the barrel, they quiver with raw energy and tannins that can range from velvety or powdery to mouth-puckering and can have more funk than a Bootsy Collins' bass line. But by the time they go into the bottle, they move with the precision of a dressage horse. And that's exactly the way Monte Bello tastes.

Snowed 2 inches, January 15, 1937. This inscription, chalked on a wall at the historic Niebaum-Coppola Winery in the Rutherford district of Napa, shows how seldom harsh weather poses a problem for wine-growers. Like Coonawarra in South Australia, the Maipo and Aconcagua valleys in Chile, or Mendoza in Argentina, California's Napa Valley is blessed with more than enough sun and warmth to ripen Cabernet Sauvignon almost every year. However, it is still a challenge to achieve the even, perfect ripeness in the grapes that give wine such as Niebaum-Coppola's "Rubicon" (left) (that Scott McLeod makes for filmmaker Francis Ford Coppola) its brilliance and weightlessness, and Warren Winiarski's "Cask 23" its kaleidoscopic beauty.

It has been said that vineyards are no more interesting to look at than potato fields. That's certainly true if you look at them with the eye of a potato farmer. Warren Winiarski of Stag's Leap Wine Cellars, at the southern end of California's Napa Valley, looks at his Cabernet Sauvignon vineyards with the eye of a gardener who understands the logic of the vine's lifecycle. He also views them with the eye of an artist, whose goal is to influence the vine in such a way that it yields grapes which precisely reflect their origin rather than just making a big, heavy wine. For him and leading Cabernet Sauvignon producers around the world, vine farming is a thing of the past and vine gardening is the new sex.

The French have always declared Cabernet Sauvignon to be one of the most ancient grape varieties, virtually a timeless original. Recently, genetic analysis has revealed this to be a myth, however, and that the vine's name is no accident. Cabernet Sauvignon is, in fact, a natural cross between the red Cabernet Franc (*see* page 112) grape and the white Sauvignon Blanc (*see* page 68). Interestingly, the characteristic aroma of ripe Sauvignon Blanc and Cabernet Sauvignon is blackcurrant, while the characteristic aromas of unripe Cabernet Franc and Cabernet Sauvignon are green veggies.

Vine gardening is the new sex

Merlot

Merlot is an easygoing and generous vine, happy-go-lucky anywhere that isn't too chilly and happy to give the wine-grower plenty of more or less ripe grapes. This, together with its reputation for being a red softy with mass appeal, has lead to ever more Merlot being planted around Planet Wine during the last two decades. Cheap, mass-produced, industrially vinified Merlot is the taste of twenty-first-century-anywhere-Planet-Wine. >>

These cramped quarters are home to one of the most extraordinary new Merlot-dominated reds on Planet Wine. Though Tertre-Rôteboeuf hails from St-Emilion in Bordeaux, whose wine-growing history goes back to the Romans, it was created by French Catalan Francois Mitjavile and his wife Miloute in 1978. It would be hard to find a wine further away from the round and plumy-tasting Merlots that fill so many supermarket shelves with the same cheerful banality that Abba dominated the charts for so many years. Unfathomable profundity and unbridled sensuality are the hallmarks of the Mitjaviles' Merlot masterpieces. "I don't believe in God, but in a wine like this you feel the power of nature," Francois says of his 1998 in the strong Leeds accent he picked up while running the UK office of his family's trucking company.

Opulent and plush without being heavy or cloying, great Merlot wines are both seductive and sophisticated. For the grape to show this side of its personality, it must grow in exactly the right conditions – which means that great Merlot is like real estate; it's all about location, location, location. Like sought-after real estate, such wines are not only expensive, but always in short supply. These limited-edition reds are hand-crafted by fanatics like Denis Durantou of L'Eglise-Clinet in Pomerol, Bordeaux, or his neighbours Belgian wine merchant Jacques Thienpont (*right*) and his British wife Fiona Morrison-Thienpont of the Le Pin estate, just down the road. Hand-crafting and the smallest differences in soil and exposition result in the contrast between L'Eglise-Clinet's firm, earthy fundamentalism and Le Pin's exoticism and silkiness.

Location, location, location

In the shadow of the long, white cloud

When Cabernet Sauvignon was unchallenged as the world's most popular grape for quality red wines during the 1980s, it got planted in all kinds of places that were simply too damp and chilly for it to ripen fully with any regularity. These puffy, maritime clouds flying over the vineyards of the Hawke's Bay region on New Zealand's North Island are the reason for Merlot's steady advance. The climate here is much better suited to it than to Cabernet Sauvignon, as Merlots such as the vibrant, rich examples produced by Ngatarawa and Redmetal Vineyards prove.

Climate is also why the Italian-speaking Ticino region in Switzerland is the scene of a Merlot revolution. Winemakers like Christian Zündel (of the eponymous estate) have seen that, given more care in cultivation and vinifcation, the grape can produce wines with a wonderful fragrance and elegance – a hundred times more attractive than the green aromas and coarse, hard taste of Cabernet Sauvignon from unripe grapes. In all senses, wines such as Zündel's "Orizzonte" are the new red wine cool.

The "Macho Merlot" style was an instant hit with wine buffs looking for a big blast, and it spread like wildfire around Planet Wine. Who does it best? That's all a question of how much jamminess and kick-boxing you can take. If you judge success by wine prices (and that is the way this type of wine is often judged by its fans), then l'Angélus, Pavie, Peby-Faugères, and Valandraud in St-Emilion, Bordeaux, are the front runners. For those without big money to burn, Casa Lapostolle and Montes Alpha in Chile provide much the same hit of flavour for a fraction of the cost.

Meet the Macho-Man, with a heart of jam

While the popularity of reds from the Merlot grape was already high a decade ago, it has taken another leap upward since then due to a new wine style pioneered in Bordeaux and beyond by flying winemakers such as Michel Rolland (whose lab is shown *left*). Their strategy for fame and fortune has been to abandon the shyness wine-growers previously showed about picking Merlot grapes overripe and tapping the grape's potential for monster wines. Making wine from overripe Merlot grapes with an inky thickness, then ageing it in 100 per cent new-oak barrels is a recipe for opulent, masssive reds that combine the subtlety of a champion kick-boxer with the sweetness of blackberry jam.

Shiraz

A great red wine from the Shiraz grape tastes as sweet and ripe as this juice looks, as it oozes from an Australian winery's ancient basket press. Totally seductive and enveloping, this is the closest red wine ever gets to liquid sex on Planet Wine. With a minimum of 14 degrees of alcohol and hardly less of any of the other things that can make red wine taste good, Shiraz is not a wine for the faint-hearted. Some examples require the drinker to be at least a demigod to live up to them. The basket press may seem a relic of the nineteenth century, but it is one of the tools of leading twenty-first-century makers of Shiraz, such as Henschke, Charles Melton, St Hallett, Turkey Flat, and Rockford (where this press is located) from South Australia. It provides the means of giving their wines a grace that enables them to slither salaciously across the palate, rather than storming it like a group of terrorists.

Unfortunately, the Oz Shiraz boom of the 1990s – the vineyard area more than tripled between 1998 and 2003 – has a downside about which little is spoken, most of all by those responsible. Intense competition for the highest prices on the market and the highest ratings from the critics drove some producers to take easy short cuts in the cellar to make their wines bigger and bolder in the body-building manner and more pouting in the *Bay Watch* sense. The equivalent of steroids and breast implants for red wine is tannin from the packet. I can't show you what this looks like because the picture has been censored. Not surprisingly, the results of the "add and stir" school of winemaking are as subtle as the pumped-up muscles of the young Arnold Schwarzenegger and about as convincing as the pneumatic curves of Pamela Anderson.

Though the grape actually hails from France's Rhône Valley, where it's called Syrah, in Australia it has achieved such a unique expression that a different name seems more than justified. In fact, in recent years, winemakers in all kinds of places around Planet Wine have been planting this vine and calling the resulting wine Shiraz, because it's the chocolate, spice, plum, and blackberry opulence of the Australian role model they seek to imitate – not the French "original". >>

Oz Shiraz: pumped up or gently squeezed?

Australian Shiraz's dazzling ascent to international acclaim during the 1990s won't turn out to be a shooting star that fades as suddenly as it appeared in the heavens, because it is based on the work of at least four previous generations of wine-growers. This is one of the first Shiraz vines to be planted in the Barossa Valley of South Australia during the years immediately following the founding of Bethaney – the oldest village in the region – in 1842 by Lutheran exiles from Silesia in Germany (now Poland). Like the music of Johnny Cash or Neil Young, the wines from these vines got better and better as they got older. Today the demand for top-quality Shiraz wines guarantees the future of these relics from the age of colonialism.

 At Mount Langhi, in the Grampian Mountains of Victoria, Australia, futurism takes the form of a vast "sail" that protects the vines from winds that would otherwise decimate the quantity and quality of the crop. Trevor Master conjures a powerful and smoky witches' brew of a red wine from the Shiraz grapes that ripen on these rugged hillsides. The extraordinary thing about Victorian Shiraz is the variety of flavour small differences in the landscape and climate can make. Jasper Hill's Shiraz from Heathcote is much more lavish and fragrant, while Best's Shiraz from old vines in Great Western, are all silk and chocolate.

The maximum force of the future

The Barossa and Clare Valleys and McLaren Vale in South Australia have almost ideal climates for the Shiraz grape. As a result, their luscious and super-succulent Shiraz wines are like blonde bombshells with "sex" written all over their faces. Anyone seeking a darker and cooler type of Shiraz beauty must leave the beaten track and explore the bush, just like the many Australian wine-growers who did so in order to explore the outer limits of this grape.

Some of the most exciting Shiraz from Australia comes from the "wine frontier", places remote from civilization. At Frankland Estate, in the Great Southern region of Western Australia, sheep, olives, and Shiraz vines flourish peacefully side by side. Then, suddenly, you'll hear the sound of a wild, thrashing engine and Mad Max shoots over the next vine-clothed hilltop. In fact, it is not a retro-fitted roadster from post-apocalyptic Australia, but ex-radiologist Judi Cullam and ex-accountant Barrie Smith's vineyard vehicle (*right*). The cool nights and long growing season here produce Shiraz with a dry elegance, a style shared by the wines from Howard Park and Plantagenet, grown nearby. They are proof that what was once a blank on the map of Planet Wine is now a space well worth watching.

Nebbiolo

Although it may look like it, this is not an exotic, new vineyard region in part of the ex-Soviet empire, the Himalayan foothills or sub-Andean Ecaudor. It's the Langhe in Piedmont, Italy, whose wines blew Julius Caesar away. It is home to the noble Nebbiolo grape, though "frustrating" and "impossible" are the words wine-growers in the Barolo and Barbaresco appellations use when the autumn mists envelop the hills and the Nebbiolo grapes are still not properly ripe. Then, there is always the real danger that heavy rains could destroy much of the crop before it is ready to pick – as the torrents of 1994 did. This fickleness is the only reason that Nebbiolo has not been more widely planted in the New World. When the grapes *do* ripen perfectly, however, it is worth all the risks and the hard work, for Nebbiolo wines have a unique palate of aromas and flavours: tar, liquorice, and roses is not an uncommon combination.

Play "Misty" for me...

Before the quality revolution that began in the Langhe during the 1970s, Barolo and Barbaresco often smelled more like salami skin and tasted as hard as nails. Since then, the winemakers of the region have learned how to avoid the harsh side of Nebbiolo and coax a charm out of the grape few suspected it possessed only a generation ago. Drinking a great modern Nebbiolo, such as the Barolos from Elio Altare, Armundo Parusso, Luciano Sandrone or Roberto Voerzio, or the Barbarescos from Angelo Gaja or Bruno Rocca, is like watching a dance of the seven veils from which a strong and curvaceous body emerges.

"If you don't like tannin, then you won't enjoy Nebbiolo" is the simple and abrupt message to the world from Piedmont's Angelo Gaja, Italy's most famous wine producer. Tannin is the stuff that makes stewed packet tea so mouth puckering, but it is also essential to a perfectly brewed, first-flush Darjeeling – arguably the noblest tea on the planet. This is exactly the contrast between slovenly made and skillfully crafted Nebbiolo wines. The winemakers of Piedmont are virtually united in their belief that the exceptionally long fermentations and barrel-ageing of the past lead to the vinous equivalent of stewed tea. But they are divided as to how Nebbiolo can best be turned into something as fine in taste as the most sought-after Darjeelings.

The Nebbiolo stairways to heaven

For two decades, the Nebbiolo winemaking dispute has revolved around the type of barrels used for maturing the young wines. Should these be the kind of "traditional" large casks of neutral wood, which Bruno Giacosa of the eponymous estate still champions, or should they be the more modern small French barriques of new French oak, that were pioneered in the region by Angelo Gaja? While it may look at first glance as if there are just two schools of Piemontese winemaking, in fact every important wine-grower has built his or her own idiosyncratic stairway to Nebbiolo heaven. And during the 1990s, many of them managed to climb ever higher towards the realm of the angelic choirs.

Grenache

Grenache seldom plays solo. Instead, it is the booming bass line that builds the foundation for some of the wine-world's greatest heavy rock. To play this role best, Grenache requires a Mediterranean-type climate with hot summers and an extreme landscape, such as the part of Châteauneauf-du-Pape with the *galet* cobblestone soil on which this dead Grenache vine has been baked by the sun. As you might expect, a grape that loves to sunbathe seldom yields wines that are light, fresh or of the quaffing type. Hugely bodied, enormosly rich wines are typical for Grenache, known as Garnacha in Spain. For all their body, however, they are seldom inky in colour or particularly fruity in character. In order to acquire those qualities, they must be blended with other grapes, as is frequently done in Garnacha's homeland of northeastern Spain, where the prefered partner grape is Tempranillo (*see* page 144). This is the recipe for the more robust style of Rioja, while in modern-style reds from the tiny Priorato area in the Penedès mountains of Catalonia, Cabernet Sauvignon is preferred. In Châteauneuf-du-Pape, Grenache is the backbone of the wine with which up to twelve other regional grape varieties are blended (Château Beaucastel often uses all thirteen), to give a wine that is as meaty, beat-y, big, and bouncy as any of The Who's early hits.

If Grenache's stock has been rising fast in recent years, it's because of the wine being made from it in contrasting regions. It would be hard to find a wine-growing region anywhere in the world that is harsher and more challenging than Priorato, on stony hillsides just below the peaks of the Sierra de Monsant in Catalonia (*left*). Compared to the vineyard workers who face this brutal environment daily, the wine-growers in the Barossa Valley and McLaren Vale of South Australia (*right*) have it easy. Although it can get just as hot there, the contours of these hills polished by hundreds of millions of years of weathering are positively gentle in comparison.

In both Spain and Australia, Grenache was a lost and forgotten treasure until the red wine boom of the 1990s kindled new interest in big, meaty reds. What enabled the comet-like rise of these wines was that, not only were they weighty, they were full of fire and wonder as well.

Burn, baby, burn!

While many rising-star winemakers are French youngsters, some of the most exciting Grenache-based wines are being made by silver-haired men and women such as Guido Jansegers, who gave up other careers for the challenge of winemaking. At Château Mansenoble, ex-insurance broker Guido Jansegers produced the first seriously powerful, elegant red wine in Corbières just a decade ago, with no prior experience of growing vines or making wine.

Though France cannot claim to be the home of Grenache, it is the place where one of the most exciting blends of red wine grapes was invented: "GSM", which stands for Grenache, Syrah (Shiraz), Mourvèdre (*see* page 128). However, the snappy abbreviation which turns the unpronounceable into the unforgettable is a classic example of Australian marketing flair. Though a great many spicy, rich, GSM reds are being produced in South Australia and Victoria, they generally play solid rhythm guitar there to the Shiraz reds' soaring lead. It is in the most dynamic wine-growing region of France, Languedoc-Roussillon, that each year GSM introduces a host of unexpected new beats to the wine world. This dynamic "New World" of French wine already has the nostalgic faction of the nation's wine establishment quaking in their boots.

Give me a **G**
Give me a **S**
Give me a **M**
what have
you got?
red joy!

WARM CLIMATE Chardonnay

Like no other grape, Chardonnay has rollercoastered from boom to bust and back again. Twenty years ago, it was *the* most fashionable grape. Then a decade later people got fed up with the butter, tropical fruit, and toasty, oaky flavours that had become the standard formula for Chardonnay and started screaming for "ABC" – Anything *But* Chardonnay. However, styles changed, the wines grew fresher, more delicate, and less oaky, and Chardonnay was "in" again. Today, wines such as the Meursaults from Domaines des Comtes Lafon in Burgundy are the object of a worldwide cult, and the absence of any sign at the estate entrance Burgundian dialect "permanently sold out".

Chardonnay is a chameleon like Madonna: one minute brash and brassy, the next glamorous and sexy, then tightly buttoned up and strict. The dry white wines produced from this grape are more responsive to winemaking – how they are pressed, how the juice is fermented, and the wine matured – than any other white grape. They can be expensive and exclusive or cheap and cheerful. It is a golden opportunity for wine designers, but also a chance for purists searching for the soul that is so easily masked with flash. The annual debut at Western Australia's premier Chardonnay producer, Leeuwin Estate in Margaret River, couldn't be more glamorous. Leeuwin Estate "Art Series Chardonnay" is serenely elegant. When this star enters the room in her long, white, backless gown, then everybody turns and stares, just as they do when Nicole Kidman makes a grand entrance.

What makes good Chardonnay such a sensually intoxicating dry white is the textural illusion that the wine is composed of many layers: in great examples they seem almost endless. Without this effect, a great white burgundy, such as the wines of Coche-Dury, Arnault Ente, Leflaive, or Mikulski, would seem a heavy, cumbersome wine – no less so than Chardonnays from California such as Kistler, Ridge, and Williams Selyem.

Fran dumb blonde to sex bomb

The deposit in the bottom of this barrel may look like gunk, but it is a vital element in the making of great Chardonnay wines. It is long contact between the young wine and its lees – the inactive and dead yeast that falls to the bottom of the barrel after fermentation – that helps weave the textural layers into the most opulent and powerful of the world's great Chardonnays. This process typically takes between six and twelve months, during which time the lees are stirred at intervals to mix them with the wine. This helps to keep it fresh and accelerates the absorption of substance and aroma from the lees. Just like the extraction of colour, aroma, and tannin from the grape-skins during red-wine fermentation, this, too, is a balancing act. Too much lees stiring, or *bâtonnage* as the French call it, can make a wine too fat and heavy: in extreme instances, it can tire it out before it even goes into the bottle. Then the process becomes entirely self-defeating. Sophie Dahl wouldn't be the sex bomb that she is if she went on hunger strike, but she doesn't need to double her body weight, either…

Chardonnay:
lees and chips
with everything

These roasted oak chips are the cheap and cheerful alternative to the rigours of barrel fermentation for Chardonnay. There is nothing wrong with them, but they will never give you the kaliedoscopic aromas and textural weave that fermentation and long maturation on the yeast in barrel does. However, that is not what the mass producers of tutti-frutti, butter-and-toast Chardonnay for the wine-store shelf are interested in. For them Chardonnay is all about push-up bra, micro-miniskirt, and follow-me shoes instantaneous appeal. Regardless of where their grapes come from they are applying a standardized, globalized winemaking formula that features plenty of chip work. It all comes down to what sort of thrill you want from your Chardonnay. If you're after a quickie then an "oaked wine" made using chips is fine, but for anyone seeking a consciousness-altering experience the only solution is a Chardonnay made in the barrel with the full winemaking voodoo.

THESEARCHFO

RELEGANCE

2 Paralleling the *über*-trend for big, fat wines oozing sweet, fruity flavours, some dazzlingly elegant alternatives developed around Planet Wine during the 1990s. They don't grab as many headlines as the Big Boys, but their advantages – they are more refreshing, more agile – mean stocks are rising steadily. One of the forces driving this trend is the expansion of cool-climate vineyards, where grapes destined for elegance can give their best. This picture shows a corner of one of the most extreme cool-climate regions: the Valais in Switzerland, where Jean-René Germanier makes a subtle red called "Cayas" from the Syrah grape. It is one of many instances of the New Elegance being discovered in wine regions with long histories behind them. There is a growing belief among winemakers that with the wines of certain grapes if you try to pump up the volume you risk blowing everything, whereas aiming to stress liveliness and harmony leads to wines of irresistible grace and danger.

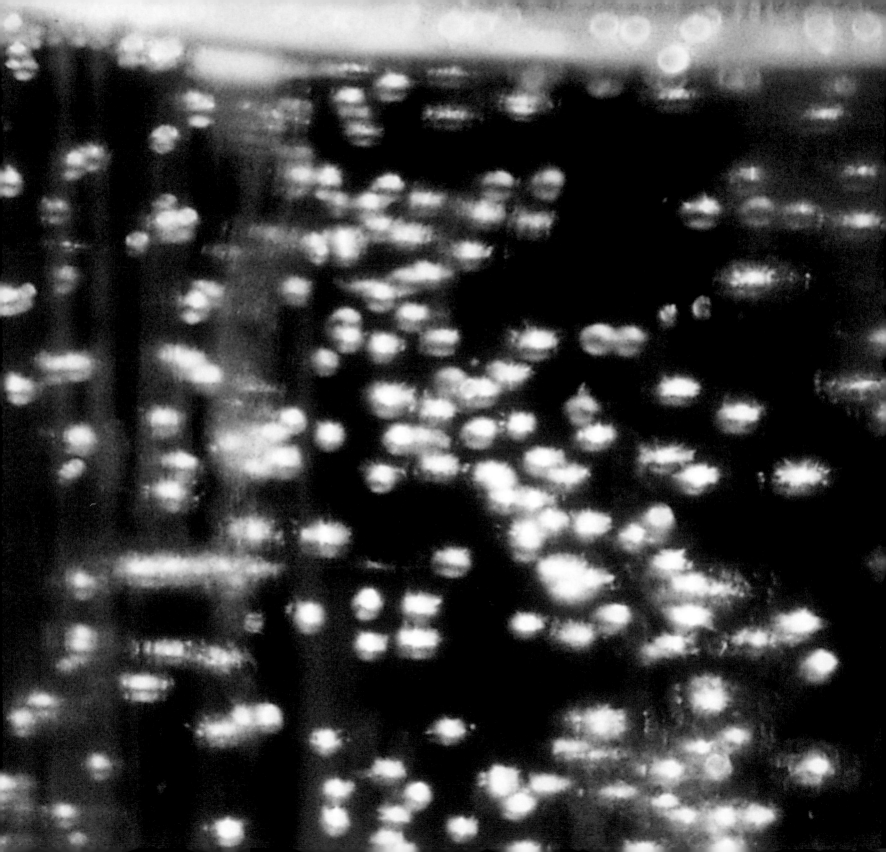

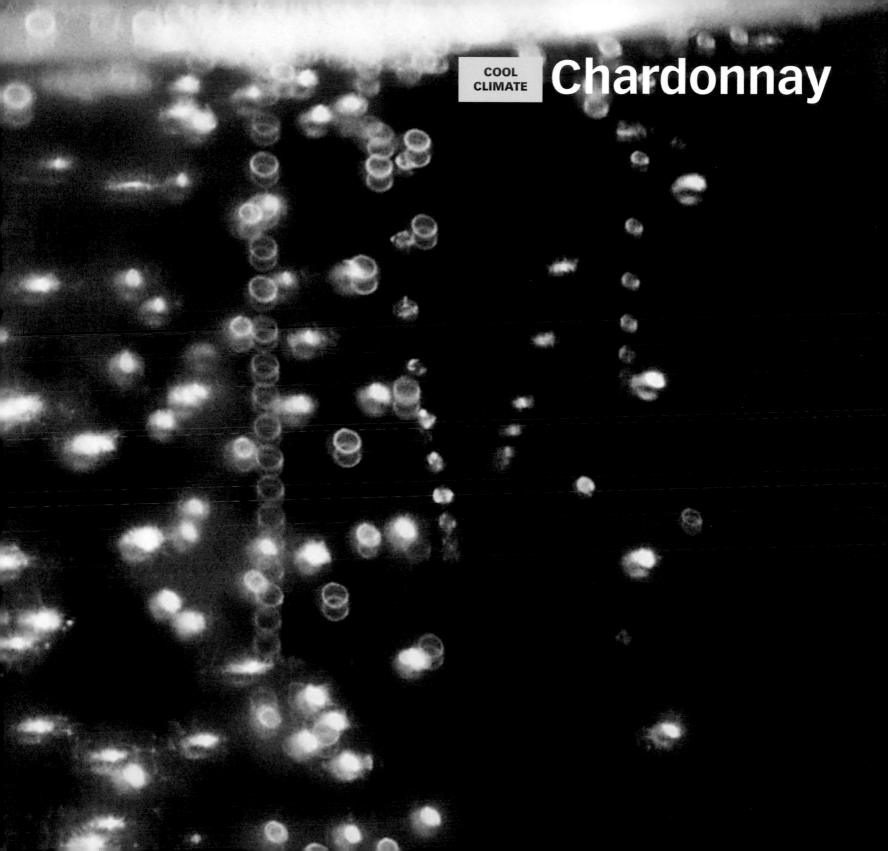

COOL CLIMATE **Chardonnay**

The least-known side of the Chardonnay grape is its ability to yield sparkling wines of devastating elegance. At once lithe and voluptuous, frivolous and captivating, with a seductive whiff of danger, the "Clos du Mesnil" from Krug is the Julianne Moore of sparkling Chardonnay *femmes fatales*. Sadly, it is also as ruinously expensive as an affair with a beautiful woman. Krug's most breathtaking rival in Champagne is the sleeker "Blanc de Blancs" from Billecart-Salmon that is as cool and unfathomable as a Hitchcock heroine. From across the waves hail the darker but no-less-compelling blanc de blancs beauties such as the generously endowed Shramsberg and the tingling tantalization of Iron Horse's "Wedding Cuvée" from California, and the Chardonnay-dominated "Deutz Marlborough Cuvée" from New Zealand – looking demure but slightly outrageous in a leopard-skin pillbox hat. While "Clos de Mesnil" comes on the market with the toasty, nutty aromas of bottle-aged Chardonnay, this is an exception. The others pose a dilemma – wait for them to gain the fine wrinkles of maturity or grab them in their sassy youth?

Michael Dhillon at Bindi, in the Macedon Ranges of Victoria, risked a climate so cool that Chardonnay can have trouble ripening fully. His "Quartz" dared to break the mould of Oz Chardonnay from day one. As its name suggests, it grows on an almost pure quartz soil and tastes supremely minerally. Currently, it is the most exciting lesson in geology Chardonnay has to teach on Planet Wine. It is also one of the most spectacular examples of how radically the Chardonnay world map is being radically redrawn today.

Sandwiched between the Neusiedler See – more a deep puddle, really, than a proper lake – and the long-closed Austrian-Hungarian border, the unremarkable wine town of Apetlon hardly looks a likely place to find one of the world's great Chardonnays. And before the Velich brothers, Roland and Heinz, produced their first vintage of Tiglat in 1991, nobody would have put any money on that number. >>

Dead cool Chardonnay

The unlikely Velich duo were not only daring, but had a feeling for the elegance of Chardonnay that most of their Austrian colleagues completely lacked at this time. Unlike their clunky, over-oaked blunderbusses, Tiglat was brimming with citrus-peel freshness and mini-banana creaminess right from its first vintage. With every subsequent harvest, it has gained in stature and subtlely, thanks to the brothers' restless striving for the ultimate.

The most exciting new white wines in France hail from the once-slumbering Mâconnais area of Burgundy, long dominated by cooperative wineries and merchants interested only in quick profits from easy export sales. Things changed rapidly, however, when a group of rebels rejected the old way of doing things in favour of a hell-for-leather pursuit of a previously undiscovered greatness they were sure could be wrought from these hills. >>

Vive la
revolution

The new radicalism of the Mâconnais often looks as unromantic as this cellar in Lugny, one of the centres of old-style mass production. Here the former forklift-truck salesman Hubert Laferrere of Domaine Saint-Denis makes some of the most startlingly pure and expressive Chardonnays in France. In Burgundy today, any white wines with pretentions to grandeur tend to get a healthy dose of oak. After experimenting with this path Laferrere rejected it in favour of working exclusively with plain, enamelled steel tanks because they enabled him to best capture the flavour of the grape. "Here, Chardonnay has enough fruit aroma not to need the barrels," he says, "I'd really like to find out if the same is true of the wines from the famous vineyards of the Côte de Beaune." For his wines it certainly works. Laferrere's Chardonnay from the village of Chardonnay having exactly the kind of restrained power and minerally elegance which the more pretentious and expensive wines of the Côte de Beaune are supposed to show, but so often don't (sadly, they all too often taste of alcohol, oak, and not much else). While most leading producers in the Mâconnais mature their wines in oak barrels for Domaine Robert-Denogent and Héritiers du Comte Lafon, it's also the taste of the grape that gives this region's wines their glorious future.

In those places on Planet Wine that nostalgically cling to outdated myths, the truth can be painfully simple. Pigott's law of French wine-growers signs says that there is an inverse relationship between the size of their signs declaring *"Ici Degustation"* and the quality of wine awaiting those unfortunate enough to accept this invitation. Other outdated wine myths can be as convincing as the body doubles used in nude scenes by famous Hollywood actors and actresses to persuade us they haven't got cellulite or a paunch.

It is a little-known fact that Chardonnay is an immigrant in the vineyard that made it famous – the Montrachet, whose eight hectares are the most expensive real estate in the Côte de Beaune in Burgundy and probably all of Planet Wine. The grape itself would appear to have originated in the village of Chardonnay, between Chagny and Mâcon to the south.

When you're in the Côte de Beaune area of Burgundy with a great white burgundy in your glass (O, bluebird of happiness where art thou!) it is tempting to believe you are in the homeland of the timeless Chardonnay grape, sister of the equally timeless Pinot Noir. What is now certain is that it is not timeless, but the result of a natural crossing of the Pinot Noir vine with an ignoble bozo called Gouais by French wine-growers. In Germany this grape is known as Heunisch because it was brought to Europe from Central Asia by the Huns when they sacked Rome!

Sauvignon Blanc

Hit the road, Jack

Although Sauvignon Blanc hails from the Upper Loire Valley in France, its international popularity has as much to do with regions as widely scattered around the globe as the South Island of New Zealand and northern California. Most of the Sauvignon Blanc wines that grow far from the grape's homeland are bolder and more expressive than the generally discreet, sleek wines of Sancerre and Pouilly-Fumé. However, what all the wines produced from this grape share is a crispness that is extremely friendly to all manner of the vegetable- and salad-dominated foods doctors keep telling us to eat. >>

The Sauvignon Blanc grape is dead easy and ultra-demanding all at once. The mind-bending challenge comes in the vineyard where growing grapes with the right mix of aromas, sugars, and acids is like trying to square the circle. But once you've achieved that miracle, then all you need to do when picking, and in the cellar, is hold onto what you've got. The boxes behind Bruce Jack of Flagstone winery in Cape Town (*below left*), along with the one under him, are his way of preventing the grapes from which he makes his flagship "The Berrio Sauvignon Blanc" from being damaged between the moment the bunches are cut from the vine in Africa's most southerly vineyard to the moment they fall into the press. Without this care the wine wouldn't have its crystalline purity or an aroma-spectrum stretching from ultraviolet to beaten gold. Batteries of stainless steel tanks may make a wine cellar look technical, but no better instrument for capturing the aromatic richness of Sauvignon Blanc has so far been found. In vineyards on the Alpine foothills in the Alto Adige region of northeastern Italy, Hans Terzer of the St Michael-Eppan cooperative (*right*) also prefers stainless steel to the oak barriques behind him. His "Sanct Valentin Sauvignon Blanc" is one of the freshest and most vivacious examples of this grape produced anywhere on Planet Wine. It mingles tropical fruit notes with full-throttle blackcurrant and has the same hyper-real sharpness as high-definition television.

It might sound bizarre to talk about dry white wine being associated with any colour except white (or at most, a pale straw-yellow), but those from the Sauvignon Blanc often *smell* as green as grass. Indeed, it's exactly this kind of in-yer-face vegetal aromas that have made New Zealand Sauvignon Blancs so popular, though the best – "Isabel", "Lawson's Dry Hills", "Staete Landt" – are brimming with ripe citrus- and some exotic-fruit aromas, too.

How green is my valley? Sauvignon green

Without any hint of grass, nettles or other members of the vegetable kingdom, a Sauvignon Blanc loses its excitement, becoming just another fresh-tasting, dry white wine (and Planet Wine has too many of those already). The problem in the vineyard is to master the breathtaking, high-wire, balancing act between greenness and ripeness. One of the places where this death-defying feat has been perfected during the last decade is the almost impossibly convoluted hill country of the Südsteiermark (South Styria), situated directly on the Austrian-Slovenian border. Here, where the Mediterranean and Continental weather systems meet, is enough sun and warmth during the day to guarantee a high level of ripeness, yet there are also enough cool, misty nights to preserve the aromas and freshness of the grape. Along with his near neighbours Alois Gross, Lackner-Tinnacher, the Polz brothers (Erich and Walter), and Willi Sattler, Manfred Tement (*left*) of the eponymous estate has mastered the art of capturing this dynamic combination in highly charged wines with multicoloured flavours of great brilliance.

There something appealingly frank about good Sauvignon Blanc dry whites, a down-to-earth take-it-or-leave-it directness to them, but they are seldom strong on mystery. Indeed, the appeal of a simple Sauvignon is about as subtle as that of a Page Three Girl – and no wine can top the unsubtle tinned asparagus smell of bad Sauvignon. It takes a wild man like Didier Dagueneau to conjure something like cinematic suspense and erotic anticipation from this frequently one-dimensional grape. He makes no secret of the fact that he stumbled once or twice along the path towards realizing his goal, but his startlingly expressive Pouilly-Fumés now provide a compelling answer to the challenge of the finest Sauvignon Blancs from New Zealand, South Africa, Austria, and Italy. They marry fabulous ripeness with great elegance and a primordial stoniness. Go Neanderthal, strike two flints together and you'll know what makes these wines so special.

A French wine critic who will remain nameless once got so excited about the fundamentalism of Dagueneau's wines that he miss-spelt the name of the vineyard site, writing "Buisson Renard" instead of "Buisson Menard". Taken with the image of the fox Dagueneau immediately changed the wine's name to be in line with the critic's mistake. Then he put an illustration of the slyest fox in literature – Goethe's Reineke the Fox – on the front label, and on the back label a poetic expression of thanks to the wine critic for the "inspired mercy" with which he abolished the wine's "unfortunate" old name. The story fits, for no Sauvignon on Planet Wine is wilder or more spicier than Dagueneau's fox.

The Loire empire strikes back

The Sauvignon Blanc vines of Pouilly Fumé in the Loire Valley have a hard enough time on the poor stony soils when they are in good health (*above*), but to realize his dream of achieving the ultimate expression of his home region's wines, Didier Dagueneau planted a vineyard whose vines he knew from the beginning would be fundamentally sick.

Each of the Sauvignon vines from which his "Asteroid" is produced will only live a few years, because, unlike almost all other European vines, they are not planted on American rootstocks to prevent the roots making a tasty meal for the phylloxera louse. These doomed vines yield only a tiny crop of super-aromatic grapes before they bite the dust.

Riesling

This is where Planet Wine literally rocks. The slate "soil" in which these Riesling vines grow on a steep hillside vineyard in Germany's Mosel Valley is a shallow layer of scree. The vines' roots plunge through this deep into the cliff face below. The Mosel is one of a dozen or so river valleys in Germany, Austria, the Pacific Northwest of America, Australia, and New Zealand where this grape yields some of the most startlingly expressive of all white wines. During the 1970s and '80s, the elegance and originality of Riesling got lost through over-commercialization and lack of care, while cheap wines hijacked the names once synonymous with its greatness. The new generation of Riesling wine-growers had to dig deep down through the detritus of opportunism, complacency, and bad habits to rediscover the lost roots of Riesling's elegance. Using minimalistic winemaking techniques, they nurture dry and naturally sweet wines in their cellars to embody James Joyce's assertion that "White wine is electricity". Clemens Bush, of the eponymous estate in Pünderich in whose Felsterrasse vineyard close this vine grows stands, is one of the quiet fanatics driving this global wine movement. Of his colleagues in this terraced section of the Mosel Valley, Reinhard Löwenstein of Heymann-Löwenstein, Andreas Barth of Lubentiushof, and Reinhold Franzen are all playing in the same league of this beautiful game.

Dare to
drink the
Bladerunner

In 1982, when the good name of the Riesling grape was being dragged through the muck by greedy wine marketers, Jeff Grosset (*right*) of Clare Valley (*left*) in South Australia began producing extraordinary dry Rieslings under his own name. At the time, he had no idea that, fifteen years later, he would be declared the leader of the Australian Riesling renaissance by the nation's media. Yet the media wouldn't have christened him thus if Grosset hadn't become a prophet of this grape's greatness and extolled its virtues unflinchingly – even when it was out in the wilderness beyond the outer limits of fashion and good taste. From the beginning, Grosset produced two dry Rieslings: one from the slate soils of Polish Hill, the other from the limestone of Watervale. They share an uncompromisingly straight and pure style, but have wildly contrasting personalities. The "Watervale" is always more succulent, generous, and open, while the "Polish Hill" is like a locked and sealed chest when young, slowly opening as it matures to reveal mineral, passion-fruit, and lime treasures. The extraordinary thing is that this is exactly how the grapes taste when Grosset walks the vineyards before harvest to assess the crop's development. From beginning to end, it is a story that is repeated throughout the Riesling world, from Germany's Bernhard Breuer of Georg Breuer in the Rheingau and Helmut Dönnhoff in the Nahe, to Emmerich Knoll in the Wachau in Austria and the Faller family – Colette and her daughters Catherine and Laurence – of Domaine Weinbach in Alsace.

At once charming and elemental, a great Riesling runs along the knife edge between sensuality and severity, extravagance and austerity. The aromatic riches that accumulate in Riesling grapes during the longest ripening season of any great wine provide the appeal; the mineral character from the soil and the grape's hallmark racy acidity crank up the tension. >>

Swiss winemaker Daniel Vollenweider looks like he might be a top DJ, but he found the naturally sweet wines of the Riesling grape from the Mosel Valley more fascinating than any other beats and followed his instinct. Not having much money of his own, he borrowed some from friends and bought vineyards on a sun-kissed hillside called Wolfer Goldgrube, which had the potential to give great wines but no reputation – and thus low land prices. *Goldgrube* means "gold-mine" in German, and although it will be many years before Vollenweider sees any significant profits from his investment, he has already harvested several crops of wines with ravishingly golden aromas since his first vintage in 2000. Vollenweider is not alone either, rather he is just one of a new breed of Riesling adventurers who learn their craft by working for established masters (in his case at Dr. Loosen of Bernkastel in the Mosel), then set out on their own with the goal of pushing the quality envelope as far as it will go. The only secrets to his success are the unswerving conviction in his goal and the determination to do whatever amount of work in the vineyard and cellar it takes to realize it. It is this uncompromising spirit which is making Riesling the brightest spot on Planet Wine's white face.

Right around Planet Wine, pioneering winemakers are prospecting for white wine gold in the form of new or forgotten vineyard locations where the Riesling grape gives wines with super-charged acidity that can outshine all-comers like Quasars do normal galaxies in the heavens. >>

Château Bela, shown a century ago in its heyday, lies in the Slovakian section of the Danube Valley. After tasting Rieslings produced here with Heath-Robinson equipment and bottled in old lemonade bottles, Egon Müller of the Egon Müller-Scharzhof estate in Germany's Saar Valley took the estate that belongs to his wife's family in hand. With the first vintage (2001) he produced a wine with richness and sophistication that tasted like the product of a famous Riesling region. How was it possible with a grape that supposedly thrives in cool climates when Bela's summers are dry and hot? Riesling is renowned as a cool-climate grape but can stand a great deal of heat as long as the nights are cool. For example, the Clare Valley in South Australia is hotter than the state's red-wine Mecca, the Barossa Valley! Bela is one of those sweet spots heading for fame in the new Riesling century.

The once and future King...

Thousands of hectares of vineyards planted with the right grape in the right place are hardly worth anything without the vision to turn those grapes into wines that please or excite. One of the secrets of the renaissance of interest in Riesling wines is the cross-fertilization of wine cultures. It was German winemaker Ernst Loosen, of Dr. Loosen in the Mosel, and J.L. Wolf in the Pfalz who provided the inspiration and know-how that enabled him and Washington State winery Château Ste-Michelle to score a direct hit with the first vintage of their joint-venture Washington State dry Riesling "Eroica", 1999. While dry Rieslings from Austria frequently have an apricot aroma (along with other aromatic riches), this new addition to the first division of this style positively oozes with apricoty succulence. No wonder many American wine-drinkers deliberately misread the label as "Erotica"…

May the Riesling force be with you

Riesling's history is a roller-coaster ride from dizzy heights to deep abysses and back again. The paradox of its dramatic recent ascent is that while German and Austrian Rieslings are the most highly esteemed around Planet Wine, it was "New World" Rieslings that rocketed the grape back towards the stars. >>

At the other cutting edge of the Riesling world lie regions such as the extreme southwest of Victoria, in Australia, where until recently there were no vineyards. However strong a language climatic statistics speak to wine experts, the proof is always in the pudding. Even today, the Crawford River vineyard of self-confessed genetic throwback John Thompson (*above*) is a tiny island of vines in a vast landscape populated mainly by sheep (many of which are his), but he has proved that Riesling can yield dry wines with world-class power and energy. Judi Cullam and Barrie Smith's crystalline Riesling from their Frankland Estate in Great Southern, Western Australia, and Stefano Lubiano's powerful, smoky wines from his vineyards in Tasmania do the same thing for their respective regions.

Harvesting any wine grape is a hectic business, but however you spell it, picking grapes for Eiswein or Ice Wine is one mad rush against the clock. It begins in the early hours of the morning and gets ever more frantic as dawn approaches. Eiswein grapes are like vampires: as soon as the sun touches them, their quality evaporates in a mist, lost forever…

Meet
Mr Freeze!

◀ ▶ Hard frost is one of the agents that can transform Riesling grapes into the the raw material for the production of dazzling dessert wines. Mr Freeze seldom elevates the grapes of other vines to anything like the same greatness. Ice wine, or Eiswein, is a rare example of international cooperation to protect a wine designation. This protection isn't only in the interests of winemakers in Germany, where Eiswein was first harvested at least two centuries ago. It is also important to leading Canadian producers such as Inniskillin (*left*), on the Ontario Peninsula, who recently made huge strides forward in Ice Wine production. On both continents, the rules of the great Ice Wine game are the same: 1) ripe grapes, because freezing concentrates whatever is in the grapes, be it good or bad, and 2) simple physics – the more extreme the frost, the more water in the berries gets turned to ice and the greater the concentration of the resulting juice. Unlike other grape harvests, torches and thick gloves are the most important equipment when it comes to picking grapes for Ice Wine – though a fast jeep for the race to the press also comes in handy. There's no guarantee that it will work, but when it does, German Eisweins (*right*), such as those from Schlossgut Diel, Dönnhoff or Emrich-Schönleber in the Nahe or Egon Müller-Scharzhof and Zilliken on the Saar, give you an idea how ball bearings in a perfectly tuned Formula One engine must feel.

Pinot Noir

No other grape drives more winemakers to the edge of madness, or even *over* the edge, than Pinot Noir. In the Central Otago region of New Zealand's South Island, Felton Road's Cornish Point Vineyard is one of the most extreme examples of this seemingly incurable form of obsession. Here at the foot of the New Zealand Alps is a patchwork of twenty-three plots. Each is planted with a different combination of Pinot Noir clone and rootstock in a daring attempt to discover the magical mix of plant material needed to conjure red wines of even more bewitching fragrance than winemaker Blair Walter and owner Nigel Greening already produce. During the last generation, the quest for the perfect Pinot has spread to the American west coast, Canada, Australia, New Zealand, South Africa, Germany, and Italy – not only because of idealism, but also because of economic forces. The world's most expensive, young red wine is a Pinot Noir: the "Romanée Conti Grand Cru" from Domaine de la Romanée Conti in Burgundy. Though most of the interesting new Pinot Noirs don't come close to matching its four-figure price tag, anyone who produces good Pinot Noir with some regularity ought to turn a healthy profit. Pinot Noir producers may have passion in their hearts and madness in their minds, but they also have dollar signs in their eyes.

Although Burgundy is the homeland of Pinot Noir and the place that proved that this grape is to red wine what the *Kama Sutra* is to sex, there was a time when many more things were going wrong here than were going right. As elsewhere in Europe, the late 1960s and '70s were a period when the wine industry was dominated by a never mind-the-quality-feel-the-width mentality, when chemical fertilizers were chucked around as if there were no tomorrow in the naive belief that crop sizes could be doubled and tripled without damaging quality. The wines of more robust red-wine grapes in other regions suffered from this rather less than the delicate and fickle Pinot Noir, whose finest qualities are easily lost without precise care of the vine and the most cautious handling of the grapes and young wines. Leading figures in the new generation of Burgundian winemakers, such as Nicolas Potel (*left*), who started his own eponymous wine company in 1997, and Cyril Audoin (*right*), who took over his family's Domaine Charles Audoin only in 2000, have found that vineyard cultivation with a goal of strengthening the vine and reducing the load of grapes it must carry has given their wines a new power and vitality. They are driven along by a bass line that is thundering and hypnotic – like that of The Who's "My Generation". And they produce wines that certainly won't die before they get old.

The whole of Central Otago is an act of daring that pushes the envelope way out. This region, which started to be planted during the 1970s, is a cool desert, situated right on the climatic edge. It is just the latest episode in story of the quest for the red wine world's Holy Grail: great Pinot Noir. It began more than six centuries ago, when wine-growers in Burgundy discovered that, when planted in exactly the right place and treated with the greatest of care, this fickle vine could yield red wines with a perfume and silkiness that were sinfully good. The struggle to achieve this goal continues there, and throughout the cooler parts of Planet Wine. >>

Pinot Noir was the first category of wine in which a positive cross-fertilization of ideas and techniques between winemakers on different continents occurred. When that started happening a generation ago, it seemed like a novel exception. Now it is becoming the norm right around Planet Wine. >>

Pinot treck: to go where no man has gone before

It was only just over twenty years ago that a small group of pioneers, led by David Lett of Eyrie Vineyards, proved that the Willamette Valley of Oregon (*far left*) was an ideal location for growing the Pinot Noir grape. But that left unclear exactly which location within the Willamette Valley was the perfect one for producing Planet Wine's slinkiest and most salacious reds. "The best sites in Oregon for Pinot Noir are still planted with Douglas Firs," says Eric Hamacher (*left*), a self-confessed ex-"crush junkie" who used to regularly circle the globe in order to work half a dozen harvests every year. He recently gave up the nomadic life and, after moving his barrels of Pinot Noir from one rented cellar space to another, finally parked them at Carlton Wine Studio, an ecologically sound collective winemaking facility that he founded together with a bunch of like-minded independent winemakers. They are the leaders of the new generation of Oregon wine pioneers whose goal is Pinot Noirs that are simultaneously true to their roots, elegant, and irresistibly sensual. They aren't afraid of sacrificing a few Douglas Firs to go where no man has gone before, since the state is blesssed with a good two million hectares of them, compared with just over 2,000 hectares of Pinot Noir vines.

The lure of producing devastating red wine beauties from the Pinot Noir grape led to the first wine-growers going intercontinental. Flying winemakers, who jet from cellars in one country to the next, may clock up a gigantic number of airline bonus miles, but they are nearly always contract workers with only one foot on the ground at any moment. A truly intercontinental vintner such as George Fromm owns vineyards on more than one side of the globe. Here he sits in front of his seventeenth century house in the historic Swiss wine village of Malans, in the upper Rhine Valley, and tastes one of his Pinot Noirs from Marlborough in New Zealand. Fromm did not hit the road in search of fame or fortune, instead, he took off on a journey of discovery in the belief that the path is the goal. It was for this reason, not to mention the fact that it lies almost directly on the main street of the Marlborough wine region, that he called his New Zealand wine estate La Strada, Italian for "The Road" (and the name of an infamous film by Frederico Fellini). The extremely generous sunshine hours make Fromm's New Zealand Pinot Noir bigger and bolder than those he makes in Malans, but the cool air from the surrounding peaks, and the warm Föhn winds that fly over them from Italy, give his Swiss Pinot Noirs a tantalizing combination of perfume and lithe strength.

The path
is the goal
of Pinot Noir

This is Russ Margach. A chiropractor from Portland, Oregon, who found that, after years of helping out at Eyrie Vineyards in McMinnville, he had suddenly become an employee there. He describes his duties at the legendary Pinot Noir producer as, "janitor, plumber, salesman, assistant to the assistant winemaker, marketing and communications, PR, etc.". That means he is founder David Lett's second in command and proves you don't have to be a trained winemaker to play attack in the first division of the Pinot Noir league.

At Stonecutter in Martinborough at the southern tip of New Zealand's North Island you ask yourself if rich and refined Pinot Noir reds can really be made in ex-dairy industry stainless steel tanks housed in sheds clad in second-hand corrugated-iron? The answer is that with a passion for Pinot Noir comparable to that of ex-environmental scientists Lucy Harper and Roger Pemberton, together with an improvisational talent on a par with theirs you could ferment great Pinot Noirs in a bathtub under a tent. By the time you read these lines Harper & Pemberton will have moved their barrels of rich and refined Pinot Noir out of the refrigerated container which was their temporary home to the new Stonecutter barrel cellar...in another shed clad in second-hand corrugated-iron.

What is it about Pinot Noir that makes ostensibly sane people give up well-paid jobs and invest money they don't have in making red wines for which they have no customers? When it is good, then Pinot Noir is an enigma that is seductive and fascinating to explore, rather than taxing to solve. And after a while you discover there is no solution at all – only endless seduction and fascination. Denise Mar Selyem and her husband Kirk Wes Hubbard founded the WesMar winery in Sonoma County in California to produce good Pinot Noirs. Having almost no money and needing to invest almost all of it in buying grapes, they rented space in an industrial ruin with peeling corrugated-iron walls. After retro-fitting it with more corrugated iron (to keep the rain and owls out) and electrical sockets and running water and they started making seductive and fascinating Pinot Noir.

Corrugated iron plus passion equals great Pinot Noir

One of the most astonishing results of vine genetic analysis is that the noble Pinot Noir is not the "original" Pinot grape, as had been supposed for centuries, but actually the bastard offspring of the rustic Pinot Meunier and the hopelessly unfashionable, but definitely upper-crust, Gewürztraminer. As bizarre as this may sound to those familiar with the wines of the parent grapes, the result of this class-crossing union is entirely logical. Pinot Meunier has given Pinot Noir its bright, berry aromas, and its up front charm, while Gewürztraminer has imparted its silkiness, extravagance, nobility, and… well, its fickleness.

Wild at heart...
in Tuscany

Tuscany may be mega-cool today, but it is actually a rugged region which only became a tourist destination after the feudal system collapsed during the 1960s and the modern world arrived. It is primarily outsiders, such as the Piemontese Paolo di Marchi of the Isole e Olena estate (*left*) in Chianti Classico, who have succeeded in civilizing the once extremely rustic and sour red wines of the Sangiovese grape. For di Marchi, this demanded the planting of new vineyards for which he had to remove *3,000 truckloads* of rock from an area just seven hectares in size. First, the land, previously a scrubby wilderness as wild as any landscape in western Europe, had to be brought under control, then the vine itself needed to be tamed. "People often say that Sangiovese wines taste astringent and sour," he says, "but if you bite into an apple and it tastes astringent and sour, then you say it is unripe." Di Marchi's first guiding principal is that, unless the late-ripening Sangiovese grape can be persuaded to

Sangiovese

ripen properly no miracles are possible in the cellar. His answer to this challenge is to plant the vineyards more densely, so that there are fewer and smaller bunches per vine. This channels more of the plant's energy into the grapes and less into lush vegetation. The result is wines that are dry and fresh, but also have a spicy mellowness and a warmth. In spite of their sophistication, they are a million miles away from "Cool Tuscany" – but they're also very close to the region's wild heart.

The Sangiovese grape can give reds ranging from light, frank, and fruity, to dark, firm, and weighty. The former used to be sold as Chianti in wicker-covered *fiasco* bottles. These have been almost completely replaced by the latter type of wine in straight up-and-down bottles during the dramatic metamorphosis the grape's wines have undergone. >>

A generous dose of media hype and a great image are helpful for any wine region, but as Chianti Classico proves, there is no substitute for the vision and single-minded dedication of individuals. Many winemakers around the world fall into the trap of thinking that if they aren't doing anything wrong, then every vintage will naturally be better than the one before, money will automatically accumulate in their bank accounts, and fame is just around the corner. Sweet dreams for the half-hearted… >>

Putting on the Sangiovese style

A hard taskmaster like the Tuscan Sangiovese grape requires an uncompromising quest for quality and the determination to do everything right, no matter what the cost. It is these qualities that have made Lorenzy Sebasti and Marco Pallanti of Castello di Ama one of the most dynamic duos on the face of Planet Wine. They judge their "Castello di Ama" Chianti Classicos against the great red wines of the world, and while they produce a number of other limited-edition reds, the focus of their endeavours is the production of several hundred thousand bottles per year of this flagship wine in an ever-better quality. Although Ama has centuries of history – nobody is quite sure just how many – its winemakers' vision is of wine as contemporary art: no less than an expression of the sun-kissed and windswept hilltops where the grapes that make it grow. Sebasti and Pallanti, therefore, decided to ornament their wine estate with contemporary art, such as an extraordinary installation by Michelangelo Pistaletto that features mirrors set lengthways into a tree trunk. "Mirror, mirror in the tree, how great can Chianti Classico be?"

When California caught onto the Tuscan Sangiovese grape during the eighties the state's gung-ho winemakers were convinced that, given a few years, they would lick the Italians at their own game, but they were in for an unpleasant surprise. In spite of all the sun and warmth, Sangiovese did not want to play ball.

Dedicated
followers
of
Sangiovese
fashion

Bill Andersen of Château Julien in the Carmel Valley of Monterey is one half of a duo of unsung Californian wine heroes. The other half is viticulturalist Marta Kraftzeck who grows the grapes for the Sangiovese wine in Andersen's pipette in a plot next door to the winery's car park. That sounds a bit crazy, but the combination of properly ripe grapes and unfussy cellar work results in wines bursting with red-cherry and plum aromas and a suppleness that Sangiovese rarely achieves, even in its homeland. They're no big deal, just really pretty and affirmative wines in a world with more than enough ugliness and negativity to go around.

When John Shafer chucked in his well-paid job in publishing to replant hillside vineyards in the Stags Leap district of California's Napa Valley he was dreaming of making great reds from the Cabernet Sauvignon grape (*see* page 24). Then he discovered the "Super-Tuscans", souped-up Tuscan reds from the Sangiovese grape and jumped in the deep end by planting a grape completely untested in his region. At first his new "Firebreak" Sangiovese vineyard looked more like a jungle and the grapes didn't want to ripen, but step by step John, his son Doug, and their winemaker Eliza tamed nature until even the Shafer dogs were happy with the result.

One of the problems with growing Syrah is that, when compared with other supposedly "noble" and "original" red grape varieties, it grows like a weed on banned growth hormones. The genetic analysis of Syrah has provided a ready explanation for this uncouth behaviour, because Syrah is the child of two French country bumpkins: Mondeuse Blanche, from the Savoie, and Dureza, from the Ardèche. Before this fact was discovered, nobody took either of the parents seriously – indeed, outside their regions, they were all but unknown. >>

Northern spirit
northern fire

Syrah

Syrah can also shine down south, particularly in places like Pic St-Loup, north of Montpellier in the Languedoc, where the cool mountain air of this craggy region reminds it of home. Here, other *émigrés* from the north, such as Olivier Briedél from Normandy, coax the most compelling combination of sleek muscularity, wild berries, and fresh mountain herbs from Syrah. Briedél's Château Lavabre is just a case in point. His red wines are among the many surprises the complex personality of Syrah has to offer – particularly off the beaten track in the "New World" of French wine.

The genius of the Syrah grape is often misunderstood when it is acclaimed as the archetypal giver of warm, generous, southerly reds, because its homeland is actually the northern part of the vineyards that line the steep sides of the Rhône Valley. A short drive south of Lyon, close to Vienne, local winemakers Yves Cuilleron, Pierre Gaillard, and François Villard recently replanted the most northerly Syrah vineyard in France on precipitously steep terraces that date back to Roman times. The resulting wine, called "Sotanum", has all the evil, smoky, and peppery beauty that has enabled Rhône Syrahs, like those from the leading producers of the Hermitage and Côte-Rôtie appellations, to cast a spell over so many wine-lovers around Planet Wine.

Though it hails from a narrow inland valley, Syrah also loves empty and remote coastlines. Places where you don't need a bunch of climatic statistics or a degree in meteorology to know that it ain't gonna be easy to ripen any kind of wine grapes there. Not that the big wine corporations would ever have discovered this fact. It was only the free spirits like Bob Lindquist, of the Qupé Winery in Santa Maria Valley, California, who first sourced grapes from vineyards in coastal valleys which regularly fill with fog from the cold Pacific Ocean. Richly textured, packed with blackberry and black-cherry flavours, spicy, and clean, these hand-made wines are the vinous equivalent of Grunge Rock: another radical West Coast art form which relied entirely upon retro-technology and "out-dated" formats.

Syrah from the madding crowd

The cutting edge of the global Syrah experiment is the Springfontein vineyard owned by Antje and Jhost Weber from suburban Essen, in northern Germany. They planted grapes among sand dunes on the coast of South Africa, close to the sleepy town of Stanford. The Webers have their work cut out keeping down the native Fynbos vegetation – and the birds, who would eat every grape. The reward is a vibrant taste of the wild New World of wine.

A Syrah planting spree that spread right around Planet Wine began with the bull market for Syrah reds from the northern Rhône in the late 1980s. Time has proved that grown in the wrong place Syrah is a weed whose wines are dumb and clunky, but in the right place it gives a witches' brew of hypnotic, red wine rhythms.

RENAISSANCEOFTH

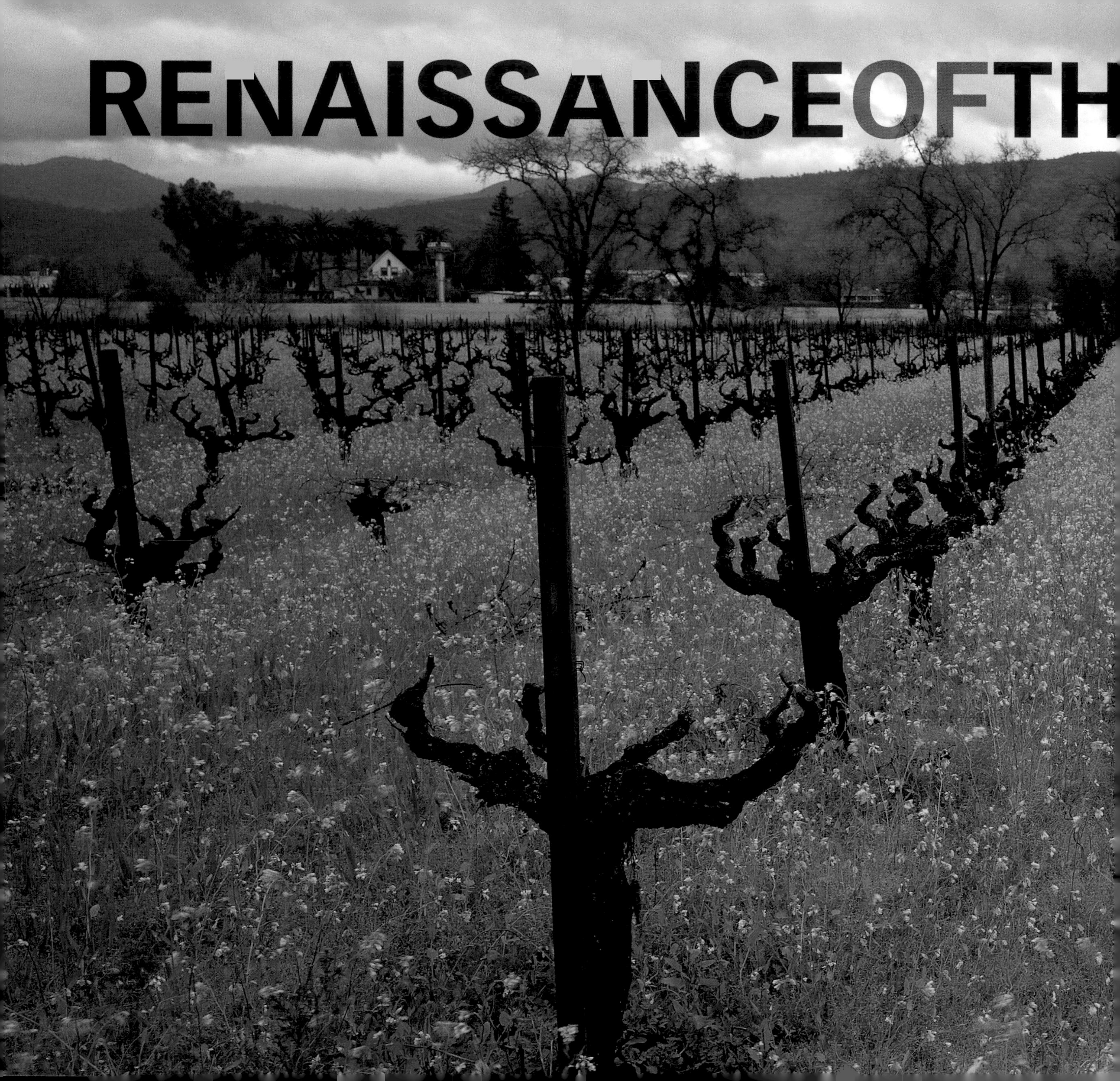

EORIGINALS

3 The laws of physics state that for every action there is a reaction. The standardization of wine caused by globalization has unleashed a backlash that grows stronger every day. For every shelf groaning under the weight of wines that smell and taste indistinguishable from one another, at least a handful of radically different wines are also produced somewhere on Planet Wine. The originality of most of these comes from the eccentric personalities of their grape varieties, turned into wine by someone with respect for their idiosyncrasies. For decades, most of these lesser-known grapes were ignored because they didn't fit into the "Big Picture" of global wine fashion. Yet the winemakers committed to them aren't interested in turning these grapes into "the next big thing". Instead, these mavericks are happy to find enough free-thinking wine-drinkers who get turned on by the wines they produce.

Assyrtiko

Wine theory states that relentless hot sun literally boils off the fruit aromas and acidity in white wine grapes that make the resulting wines refreshing and energizing. However, if there is one rule on Planet Wine then it is that there are no rules. Assyrtiko, a grape indigenous to the Cycladic islands of Greece, can stand any amount of sun and drought and still yield dry white wines, brimming with vibrant honeysuckle and lemon aromas and a crispness reminiscent of wines from far cooler climes. Nowhere is the result more astonishing than on the volcanic island of Santorini, which in 1520 BC was torn apart by a gigantic explosion that many believe was the origin of the legend of the lost continent of Atlantis. Here, Sigilas and Gaia produce Assyrtiko wines that are utterly modern in their clarity, but primeval in their expression. Their startling vibrancy and intense mineral flavour make you feel as if you can taste the bare rock in which the vines roots seek water and nourishment.

The Roman Emperor Hadrian once remarked that "Wine introduces us to the volcanic mysteries of the soil." He would have understood Assyrtiko wines instantly.

When Leon Karatsalos and his partner Yannis Praskevopoulos launched the first vintage of Gaia Estate in 1997, it instantly raised the standard for reds made from the indigenous Greek Agiorgitiko grape. Instead of the blunt astringency long typical of Agiorgitiko, Gaia managed to entice damson and vanilla aromas out of it and wraps its iron tannins in a velvet glove.

Agiorgitiko

The secret behind this dramatic change lies first of all in a vineyard in the mountains of Nemea 650 metres (2,132 feet) above sea level. Then in the kind of cosseting of vine, grape, and wine that was previously unknown in this country's long wine history. The Gaia Estate reds' almost instantaneous international success proved that new reds don't have to have an identikit soft and gooey style in order to score a direct hit with wine-drinkers and the media around Planet Wine. Nor do successful wines need to come from grape varieties with familiar monosyllabic names. All they need is the kind of strong personality of Agiorgitiko, plus harmony, and an appealing presentation like Gaia Estate's. Today the inhabitants of Planet Wine dwell in possibility: a fairer house than production, more numerous of windows, superior for doors.

Barbera

Every picture tells a story, but some tell better tales than others. This pair speaks of *metamorphosis*. First, we have the almost total transformation of the Piemontese Barbera grape achieved within a couple of years by Giacomo Bologna. Second, there is the way in which the new-style Barbera he created changed his life.

Beyond
all
expectations

The Barbera Giacomo Bologna is tasting in the photo from 1963 (*right*) does not deserve a better glass because it is rough stuff. Pale, tart, and slightly spritzy, this kind of Barbera was OK for quaffing – if nothing else was available. No wonder Piemontese vintners regarded Barbera as the most inferior of their indigenous grapes. In the photograph from 1983 (*left*), however, Bologna draws a sample of his revolutionary 1982 "Barbera Bricco dell'Uccellone" from a new-oak barrique for his daughter Raffaella. Although the wine in this photo is not yet a year old, Bologna radiates a completely different kind of confidence, because this red "was beyond all expectations". Dark in colour, rich in texture yet fresh and animating, it was the first "New Wave" Italian Barbera. Not only did it make Bologna and his Braida estate famous, but it also instigated a glorious revolution that has become the contemporary competition among Piemontese winemakers to out-do one another with this once humble grape. Elio Altare, Corino, Armundo Parusso, and Giorgio Rivetti's La Spinetta are the other front runners in this race.

Blaufränkisch
Kékfrankos
Lemberger

Drinks
    with wolves

In Germany, Blaufränkisch is known as Lemberger. It's widely cultivated in the Württemberg region, where a group of young winemakers, headed by Rainer Wachtstetter, are rescuing it from erstwhile anonymity as a nameless blending component. In its native Hungary, where it is called Kékfrankos, it is also experiencing a revival – for good reason.

Blaufränkisch yields strikingly different wines depending upon where it is grown. Warmer areas coax darker, more chocolatey tones; while cooler climes result in herbal freshness and a call-of-the-wild raciness. "Which grape varieties is your Perwolf made from?" the French wine merchant's translator demanded

of wine-grower Reinhold Krutzler of south Burgenland, Austria. The translator expected to be told how one or more of the "classic" French grapes was responsible for Perwolf's quality and style. "Lots of Blaufränkisch," Krutzler answered. "Then some more Blaufränkisch – and then a little more Blaufränkisch…" "Yes, but there's Cabernet

Sauvignon in it, too: *lots* of Cabernet Sauvignon!" retorted the translator. She should have noted the wine's sour-cherry aroma and its appealing hint of tartness. Krutzler held up his right hand, the tip of his index finger 0.5-cm (0.2 in) from the tip of his thumb. "And *so much* Cabernet Sauvignon," he said, smiling.

Not only does the Austrian Blauer Zweigelt grape suffer from being burderned with a tongue-twisting name, it also has what could politely be called a "chequered history".

This euphemism means that, for a long time, it was grown almost exclusively for the mass production of red wines sold in ugly two-litre bottles called *Doppler* (in which similarly basic whites were also sold). When the nation's red wine renaissance began during the 1980s, Blauer Zweigelt got brusquely pushed aside by ambitious young winemakers in the rush to plant French grapes, most importantly Cabernet Sauvignon which was then mega-cool. Now, many of those same winemakers are turning their backs on the French immigrant having found that, in their climate, it seldom lived up to its image. And they are replanting Zweigelt. They discovered that when reined in rather than encouraged to fill *Doppler*, it not only yields a strong, fleshy wine with spicy, peppery aromas and tasty tannins, but makes the ideal core of blends with other Austrian and French red wine grapes. None of the latter are more imposing than Josef Umathum's "Hallebühl". No varietal Zweigelt is more joyfully fruit filled than that made by Paul Achs (*below, left*).

Dig the blues

Blauer Zweigelt

As a solo act Cabernet Franc is uncommon, but in the Villány-Siklós region of southern Hungary, close to the Croatian border, a group of local winemakers have found that it gives them even more expressive and longer-living wines than either imported Cabernet Sauvignon or the indigenous Kékfrankos. Rustic as this world may look at first glance, the Mondivin Cabernet France made by Ede Tiffán proves that it is capable of remarkable refinement. It has a subtle spiciness which, along with the fragrance of violets and a discreet tartness, is the hallmark of the ladyrocker of grapes.

The many faces of the goddess

After being reduced to a supporting role by its precocious progeny, Cabernet Sauvignon, Cabernet Franc's originality is being rapidly rediscovered by a new generation of winemakers around Planet Wine. They fell in love with Cabernet Franc and are giving it star billing.

Cabernet Franc

When Cabernet Franc is an equal partner in blended reds such as the mind-blowingly dense yet fragrant "Maya" and "Viader" (with Cabernet Sauvignon, *see* pages 24–33) from California's Napa Valley, or the weightless intensity of "Château Cheval Blanc" (with Merlot, *see* pages 34–9) from St-Emilion in Bordeaux, it gives them a devastating elegance. Taking the Cabernet Franc out

of them would be like stealing the high heels and low-cut gowns from a trio of movie divas immediately before Oscar night. In less stratospherically expensive St-Emilions, the grape is responsible for a light-footedness and *joie de vivre* that prevents even powerful, assertive wines like Bordeaux wine-goddess Christine Vallet's "Château Troplong-Mondot" from tasting bombastic or ponderously buxom.

MERLOT

Carmenère

"We thought we had two clones of the Merlot grape," Eduardo Chadwick of Chile's Errázuriz estate explains. "Then, in 1994, we discovered that the better of them was not Merlot at all, but a grape we had never heard of before called Carmenère. In 1997, this was confirmed by DNA analysis." Merlot is one of the fashionable grapes of the 1990s' wine boom (see pages 34–9) and Carmenère is an ancient variety from Bordeaux, where it was widely cultivated during the eighteenth century before being squeezed out by Cabernet Sauvignon during the nineteenth. Today, just fifteen hectares of Carmenère are planted in Bordeaux because it's so difficult to cultivate. The size of the crop shoots up and down, and the grapes must be completely exposed to the sun during the final ripening phase if the wine is to taste of something other than green capsicum. When Carmenère reaches full ripeness though the green capsicum aroma becomes that of red capsicum, and with oak maturation that becomes roasted red capsicum. Combined with the black-cherry or blackberry fruit and generous tannins the grape can also pump out, this makes for bold and hedonistic reds. The potential of Carmenère is only just beginning to be grasped in Chile and looks set to at least equal that of any other grape there. Watch this space for a major feature coming to your neighbourhood soon!

Carmenère was almost lost in its homeland until wine-growers on the other side of Planet Wine unexpectedly pulled it back from the brink.

Can you taste the real Me?

Chenin Blanc

Stolen French kisses

Here it is, the all too predictable clichéd image of dry white Chenin Blanc from the Loire, those timeless castles in one of Old Europe's most picturesque tourist traps. Physically, they are almost as far as you can get from the vineyards high up on the Phurua Plateau in Northearn Thailand from which some of the most exciting new dry Chenins are coming. The savannah-like landscape there is also about as far removed from the verdant valleys of western France as you can get, yet the all-Thai team at Château de Loei lead by Oraem Terdpravat, is proving that you don't need centuries of tradition to make vibrantly fruity and wonderfully crisp dry wines from this grape. Château de Leoi's first vintage was 1995, but she and "the boys" have already proven that the combination of a remarkable climatic niche and perfectionism makes Chenin wonders possible.

Thankfully for wine-lovers, Croatian Mike Dubrovic (*right*), of Mulderbosch in Stellenbosch, South Africa, was not satisfied with the pump-it-out-cheap policy typical of his colleagues when it came to making wines from Chenin Blanc. Instead, he created his own utterly distinctive style of dry Chenin, where the grape's happy-go-lucky apple and pear fruit was given an audacious French kiss of wood. When the brazen youngster hit the local wine market a decade ago, it was a runaway success, leading to dozens of imitators. It encouraged other daring South African winemakers, such as David Trafford of de Trafford, to push this form of French kissing even further.

It was the Chenin Blanc grape's bad luck to have long been treated as the vinous equivalent of Muzak: mindless, off-dry white stuff for so-called "easy drinking". It has been planted at all points of the compass, starting in its homeland in the Anjou region of France, then ranging from northern Thailand to South Africa to California. Yet, until recently, exciting dry Chenin Blanc was a rarity anywhere.

Furmint

The name of the Furmint grape rarely appears on the labels of the wines for whose greatness it is primarily responsible. Instead, these declare their region of origin – Tokaj, Hungary – with the greatest pride. During the postwar period, however, there was little for local wine-growers to be proud of. Forced collectivization, the Communist obsession with production figures, and the paucity of interested consumers led to the steady erosion of the 400-year-old culture of Tokaji wines, the Furmint-dominated dessert wine.

Thankfully, since the fall of the Iron Curtain, everything in Tokaj has changed. Today, when the mists roll down the Bodrog Valley during the autumn, bringing the noble rot that concentrates the Furmint grapes and aromatically transforms their juice, a whole pack of new winemakers is waiting to grab the opportunity presented by the *Aszú*: the botrytis-shrivelled grapes and also the wine made from them. Aside from any stylistic differences, the goal of all these winemakers is the same – to make the equivalent of the Countess of O in dessert wine form: a wilful and domineering beauty, at once strict and hedonistically decadent. No Tokaji Aszú wines manage this act of erotic daring act better than those from István Szepsy's own estate and the Királyudver winery he directs. However, the *aszú* wines from Disznókö and Oremus are only slightly less unrelenting in their whiplash-like brilliance.

The strictness of mistress aszú

Garganega

The name of the main grape variety – Garganega – that went into these wines was not printed on the label, or else it, too, would have been dragged into the mire. Though Soave can boast a handful of producers who believe in Garganega's potential to produce white wines with a distinctive character, none has revolutionized the area's wines like the Pieropan family. Nino and Teresita, together with their sons Andrea and Dario, grow their Garganega grapes exclusively on the hills where the vines must struggle, rather than down on the plains where they have an easy life and regularly fill those huge tanks with blah-blah-blah Soave. The result of their endeavours is a joyful, extrovert wine in which the floral aromas of spring mingle with the ripe fruits and fresh nuts of autumn – and there's not even a hint of blah-blah-blah. Now the people of Planet Wine can choose between one-chord-wonder Soave and polyphonic Pieropan.

All over Planet Wine you hear the same story: how the vicious circle of negligence and poor quality was broken by daring pioneers whose startling new wines were the products of self-criticism and dedication to goals other than an easy life and quick profits. Take Soave. It used to be synonymous with all that was wrong with Italian white wines – huge concrete tanks overflowing with bland, watery wine destined to fill the crude glasses in a thousand dingy pizzerias.

The beginning
of the end of
blah-blah-blah

Powerful, white magic

Tired, bland, and dreary was how most Mediterranean whites tasted before the arrival of modern cellar technology. Fresh, bland, and dreary is how most of them taste today. However, slowly those grapes with the potential for white wine lightning in these warm climates, such as the Fiano of southern Italy, are being discovered, and the white wine times in the Mediterranean finally are a-changing.

During the 1990s Southern Italy became a Mecca for dynamic red-wine producers, but the dry whites remained stubbornly turgid and dull the vinous equivalent of a third-rate heavy-metal band missing the beat and playing slightly off-key. Then a handful of young winemakers, including no-names like Luigi Maffini, began making startlingly bright and lively tasting whites from an ancient indigenous grape variety called Fiano. While none of these have gone platinum yet, Maffini's "Kràtos" from the steep terraces on the coast of the Cilento Peninsula, south of Naples and the Planeta family (*right*) of Sicily's "Cometa" have made the first league of Italian whites. "Kràtos" has a honey and pineapple fragrance that makes it taste fresher than many northern whites which benefit from northern lightness. "Cometa" pulls off the trick of marrying lushness and creamyness with a vigour so rare for Mediterranean whites.

Fiano

Gewürztraminer

◀ Although Klaus Zimmerling's Gewürztraminer grows on the southern outskirts of Dresden, close to the fifty-first parallel, there is nothing icy about its beauty. Instead, it has another kind of coolness than Foradori's (*right*): a northern freshness that enables it to pack a big punch of flavour and alcohol from Dresden's hot, dry summer without tasting heavy or flabby. Zimmerling (*left*) prefers female company when he drinks his rich but bone-dry Gewürztraminer – which not only means his wife, Polish artist Malgorzata Chodakowska, but also her sculptures. Interestingly, Germany's other great Gewürztraminer producer – Rebholz, in the Pfalz – has already discovered that his slightly sweeter, more opulent Gewürztraminers taste pretty good drunk with Chodakowska's women, too – but her work is unfortunately hundreds of times more expensive than any of these equally entrancing wines.

The other name
of the rose

It was just a coincidence, but one of those coincidences that look like destiny. Suddenly the leading Alto Adige winemakers in northeastern Italy found that their fastest-selling wine was dry Gewürztraminer. Only a decade before, wines from the same grape lay in their cellars like lead. Around the same time, genetic analysis revealed the astonishing truth that not even the most crazed Gewürz fan would have dared consider: this grape is the prime souce of the nobility of European grape varieties, ranging from Cabernet Sauvignon and Pinot Noir to Chardonnay and Riesling.

What none of Gewürztraminer's numerous progeny among the "classic" grape varieties have is that quality that gives a great dry Gewürz its sultry beauty: the enveloping perfume of yellow roses. This is a grape whose signature aroma is devastatingly obvious to anyone who can remember what roses smell like. At least when it comes to their fragrance, Gertrude Stein was wrong when she wrote that "a rose is a rose is a rose", for if you compare them, different roses smell quite different – just as different Gewürztraminers do. The "Kolbenhof Gewürztraminer" produced at J. Hofstätter by Mr Cool-Italian-Wine Martin Foradori in the Alto Adige region, (*above*) has *A Midsummer Night's Dream* of a rose aroma that makes it more of a trance wine than something to drink to Foradori's beloved drum 'n' bass. In it, alpine freshness and Mediterranean warmth embrace one another.

Grüner Veltliner

Unlike the mass of amiable but run-of-the-mill dry Grüner Veltliners, Willi Bründlmayer's version, from the Lamm vineyard of Langenlois, in Austria's Kamptal region, is a wine of immense proportions, yet at once clean and caressing. In more recent years, during a series of blind tastings held in London, New York, and Vienna, it repeatedly trounced what are commonly supposed to be the elite dry white wines of France (specifically Burgundy), Europe, and the world. To make top dry GVs like Willi Bründlmayer or Bernhard Ott (*right*) of Feuersbrunn in the Donauland, you mustn't be afraid of alcohol or opulent richness – or of aromas like white pepper and tobacco that are far off the usual dry-white scale. *Der Ott* – literally "The Ott" – is what the Fatboy Slim of Grüner Veltliner calls the most elegant of his sledgehammer wines. It is exactly this breed of Grüner Veltliner that is redrawing the white wine map of Planet Wine.

Get a hit off the elegant sledgehammer

No white grape has gone faster from next to nowhere to international stardom than Grüner Veltliner, the most widely planted grape in Austria. The wines that kept GV out of the limelight for so long were the light, crisp, dry whites with a touch of pepper that account for the pleasant but unspectacular bulk of production. Compared to these, the GV wines which are now winning over the world taste as if they come from a different star.

Malbec

When it arrived in Argentina from its native Cahors
in France, the thick-skinned Malbec grape underwent
an unexpected transformation.

Instead of letting its hair grow and going native after emigrating from southwest France to Argentina, this robust and often rustic grape progressively lost all its rough edges and acquired civilized manners on the slopes around Mendoza, at the foot of the Andes. During the 1990s, the Catena estate really showed what a suave and elegant wine this variety could turn into when grown high enough so that the mountain air enabled the grapes to ripen without being burnt by the sun. It wasn't long before other producers, such as Fabre Montmayou and Norton, were following suit. Partly because that pair of wineries are French owned, news of these developments got back home to Cahors, to a fanatical young *vigneron* called Pascal Verhaeghe (*above*) of Domaine du Cèdre, who was already making Cahors that were unashamedly modern in their clarity and authentic in their directness. Not that he decided to imitate the successes of the competition from the other side of Planet Wine, however. No. He was determined to create Cahors' answer to them. His "Le Cèdre" is a dark and spicy, mouth-puckering, take-no-prisoners Cahors classic you couldn't mistake for anything else. If you're strong enough to cope with the results of Verhaeghe pumping up the volume as far as it will go on the Malbec scale, then his spicy masterpiece is one hell of a beautiful monster!

Perhaps it should come as no surprise that this red grape seems to exert a fatal attraction upon crazed winemakers. Here is Randall Grahm of Bonny Doon in Santa Cruz, California, making life imitate art by acting out the label of one of his wines. Under his "Euro Doon" label, he produces a Tannat from its home region of Madiran, in southwest France. It's called "Heart of Darkness" after Joseph Conrad's novel, which in turn formed the basis of Francis Ford Coppola's Vietnam film *Apocalypse Now*. In fact, while dyed-in-the-wool Madiran is the vinous equivalent of Mr Conrad's Colonel Kurtz (or the napalm attack scene in Coppola's film), Grahm's interpretation of the hard man of red wine grapes turns it into a bit of a dish. Somehow Mr Surf-Wine USA has managed to coat its earthy, butch soul in a sweetness that makes it positively pretty. Cult Madirans like Château Montus may make a bigger noise, but they are often calculating and pretentious. The "Dayman" Tannat made by Denis Duveau at Castel La Puebla in Uruguay is much closer

to the spirit of Grahm's creation. In 1992, Duveau left his native Loire for South America to experiment in an atmosphere freer than that of France. "Most producers grow Tannat in the south of the country," he explains, "but that's only to be close to the port. Tannat needs an enormous amount of sunshine in order to shine, which is what makes the Dayman Valley ideal." It wraps the aromas of wet clay and hot tar in a rich and tannic package, that is dangerously handsome.

Mad, bad, and dangerous

Wine grapes don't come much crazier than the tannin-bomb that is Tannat.

Tannat

Mourvèdre
Mataro

I just can't resist your animal magnetism

Mourvèdre – or Mataro, as it's called in Australia and California – is a red grape that does not really want to play ball. Yet when it turns out right, the result is a red wine with tremendous animal magnetism: a funky charisma that'll either turn you on or leave you stone cold. The biggest problem for this incorrigible sun-lover is that the grapes often ripen extremely unevenly. You can see which grapes are good (black) and which are just sour (green) at first glance (*left*), but often Mourvèdre makes the winegrower's life hell. "Some years I have to taste every single bunch in order to decide if it's good enough to use or not," grumbles Château Mansenoble's Guido Jansegers, in Corbières, southern France (*see also* page 54).

Animalistic aromas in red wines – sweaty leather, stables, elephants' feet – usually result from a lack of basic cellar hygiene, but some red wine grapes manage to smell of pelts and hides even without the help of a slovenly winemaker. None more so than funky Mourvèdre.

There's no simple solution to Mourvèdre's bad behaviour, however, it does seem to create the sexiest wines when it not only gets plenty of sun, but can also see the sea, as in Bandol, in Provence. Here, the grape frequently gets ultra-ripe due to a very long, warm, growing season that gives the resulting wine a fleshiness to cover its big and sometimes bony frame. When this happens, you get wild and luscious, dashing hulks like "Château Pibarnon", "Château Pradeaux", and "Château la Rouvière". Although statistically it usually plays the smallest role, Mourvèdre gives many GSM reds (Grenache, Syrah [Shiraz], Mourvèdre; *see* page 54) the animalistic kick that makes them outrageously original, rather than just wine fashion items.

Muscat Blanc à Petits Grains
Muskateller
Moscato

Who's that grape hanging around with you?

Many aromatic grapes tend to yield heavy, cloying wines, but a great dry Muskateller, such as those which Hansjörg Rebholz of the Rebholz estate in the Pfalz, Germany (*right*), are at once explosively aromatic yet almost weightless, with the crystalline clarity of a mountain stream. At the other end of the earth – and at the golden end of this grape's wide aromatic spectrum – lies the dense, unctuous, yet staggeringly fresh "Vin de Constance" dessert wine from Klein Constantia of Cape Town, in South Africa. Made from grapes that shrivel and darken on the vine (*left*), it captures every flavour nuance of this variety: from just ripe to the moment before the raisined berries collapse completely to become black holes.

Some wine cults are all about money, scarcity, status – in essence, vanity. The Muscat cult is the opposite – a common obsession with one of the most chronically underrated of all wine grapes. Those who think wine only intoxicates because of its alcohol have never tasted a great wine from the most noble of this wide family of grapes. Muscat Blanc á Petits Grains (in France), Muskateller (in the German-speaking world), or Moscato (in Italy), its decadently grapey bouquet is the most addictive currently unlisted drug I know.

Nero d'Avola

The recent "gold rush" in Sicily was sparked by the global red wine boom, but those sparks wouldn't have ignited a wildfire of new plantings had it not been for the indigenous Nero d'Avola grape. The reliably hot and dry climate here is predestined for the production of big, rich reds of exactly the kind that are the hottest wine style internationally. However, most of the grape varieties imported to the island have found the climate to be too much of a good thing: their wines often turned to lead or flab in the heat.

Drink the
black gold
of the sun

Nero d'Avola relishes Sicily's climate of extremes, without which it would be unable to give the world so many big, black beauties with aromas as bewitching as a voodoo love potion. It's hard to believe that just a decade ago this potential was almost completely unrealized, and most Nero d'Avolas were sullen or thunderous. Now the grape's name is a buzz word and it has a growing cult following at home and abroad, but experience suggests that its full glory has yet to be smelt and tasted. Only recently have some Nero d'Avolas edged up into the double-figure price bracket where the money necessary for intensive vine and grape cosseting becomes available, but their number look set to increase. Then we can expect to drink the black gold of the sun.

It was star oenologist Riccardo Cotarella (*right*) who first turned this grape into red-wine gold at the Morgante wine estate. Though Morgante's "Don Antonio" set the pace for the new wines, the regular bottling, named after the grape, is one of the rare examples of a currently endangered species on Planet Wine: red wine bargains. At the head of the leading pack of Nero d'Avola specialists are the Di Gaetano family of Firriato with their uncompromisingly I-am-what-I-am Nero d'Avola hunk called "Harmonium". For all its humongous opulence and alcohol, it is as harmonious as its name suggests.

In its home region of Bordeaux, France, Petit Verdot either falls short of the target or lands bang in the middle of the black. The reason why this is an all-or-nothing wild card for the wine-grower is its dangerous habit of late-ripening in a climate where autumn is virtually synonymous with Atlantic storms. No wonder nobody in Bordeaux risks planting more than ten per cent of their vineyards with it…

Petit Verdot

Petit Verdot's recent rise to prominence is the result of wines grown in less-risky climates than its French homeland. At Castello dei Rampolla in Chianti, Tuscany, Alceo di Napoli became the first to risk planting a substantial area with this variety during the late 1980s. However, it was not until a full decade later, after his death, that his son Luca and daughter Maurizia (*right*) were able to release the first "La Vigna di Alceo", in which Petit Verdot and Cabernet Sauvignon are blended half and half. It's the intense blackberry aromas and electric acidity of the Petit Verdot that give this wine its head-turning and mind-jolting energy.

Carlos Falcó, also known as the Marqués de Griñón, planted Petit Verdot at his Dominio de Valdepusa estate close to Toledo, Spain, in order to blend it with other red bordeaux grapes, yet he found it so exciting by itself that he started bottling most of the production as a varietal wine. At once black and fresh, muscular and elegant, it's the Grace Jones of Spanish red wines – and like her, not afraid to show plenty of flesh.

Pinotage

Pinotage is the product of the 1925 crossing, by Professor
Perold of Stellenbosch University, of the noble Pinot Noir grape
(*see* pages 84–93) of Burgundy with the southern French hobo
Cinsault. Cultivated with quality rather than quantity in mind,
it tastes like a gonzo Pinot Noir, but try and pump up the size
of the crop and its rustic roots show through in coarse and
astringent flavours that have earned it a bad reputation
among wine snobs.

"What other powerful red
wine is so harmonious that
you can drink it from its earliest youth?"
Joachim Krige of the Kanonkop estate,
Stellenbosch, asked rhetorically. To prove
his point, he scooped some fermenting
Pinotage out of one of the troughs, where
workers were "punching down" grape-skins
into the embryonic wine. Though it looked
exactly like th picture (*left*), I took a big gulp
and found that it was bizarrely tasty. Hot on
its heels followed a sample from a tank just
two weeks older. I drained the glass of this
richly herbal witches' brew. Only Pinotage,
the sole indigenous South African grape,
makes this miracle possible.

Pinot Blanc
Pinot Bianco
Weissburgunder

Pinot Blanc is the victim of a self-fulfilling prophecy. Because most "experts" consider it to be a second-class citizen among grapes, most winemakers don't give it the attention it deserves. Mostly it fails to achieve the greatness of which it is capable – thus confirming the "experts" judgement.

The Pinot Blanc grape suffers from standing in the mighty shadow cast by its close relative, Chardonnay. Chardonnay might sometimes be the dumb blonde of Planet Wine, but it is also the grape from which white burgundy and many sought-after dry whites from elsewhere are produced, giving it stacks of glamour. What does its poor cousin have to offer in comparison to that? Well, for starters, this grey mouse gives an enormous number of pleasant dry whites for everyday drinking (from Alsace in France; northeastern Italy; the Rheinhessen, Pfalz, and Baden in Germany). Then there are the undiscovered masterpieces made by unlikely heroes. Making great Pinot Blanc is all about finding special climatic niches where the grape can reach a staggering ripeness without losing freshness, then – in complete contrast to Chardonnay – doing as little as possible to the wine in the cellar. Given this, time and tide coax amazing fruit aromas and a feline agility out of the wine that make most Chardonnays taste like Identikit fashion victims with big hair and push-up bras. Ripe apples and pears, peaches, and pineapples are the main facets of Pinot Blanc's fruit extravagance, but it is when these riches are crowned with a whiff of fresh hazelnuts that Pinot Blanc is transformed no less dramatically than the normal secretary played by Michelle Pfeiffer who turns into Cat Woman in Tim Burton's film *"Batman's Return"*.

Rainer Bergdolt and his daughter Caroline (*left*) of the Bergdolt estate in the German Pfalz are both fanatical believers in Pinot Blanc – called Weissburgunder in their region. Their wines from the Mandelberg vineyard, close to sleepy Duttweiler, are amongst the most powerful and energetic dry whites on Planet Wine. However, all their strength is reined in and their "Lebensfreude" is anything but loud compared with what the French usually mean when they speak of *joie de vivre*.

From another Pfalz vineyard, also called Mandelberg, Karl-Heinz Wehrheim (*right*) of the Dr. Wehrheim estate conjures Pinot Blancs from rocky slopes, high up near the jagged peaks of the Haardt forest, with herbal and mineral aromas of kaleidoscopic complexity.

Neither these nor other top Pfalz Weissburgunder like Müller-Catoir, Münzberg, and Rebholz need anything more fancy than a few stainless steel tanks and a lot of patience to make super-heroine Pinot Blanc.

Cat woman in white

Pinot Gris
Pinot Grigio
Grauburgunder

White wine
warp nine

The greyness in the Pinot Gris name comes from the violet-grey colour of the skins of this grape. Not surprisingly, a bad example can taste exactly that way: terminal bland-out. Sadly, that's all too common in northeastern Italy (where the grape is called Pinot Grigio), Alsace (France), and in Rheinhesssen, Pfalz, and Baden in Germany (where it is called Grauburgunder) – that is, in all the main wine-growing regions this variety frequents. The reason for this is the current global thirst for dry white wine that tastes utterly inoffensive: fresh, yet as soft as butter. Overcrop Pinot Gris and that's exactly the kind of alcohol-water solution you get. Tasting a great Pinot Gris like those from the Dr. Heger estate's vineyards in the Kaiserstahl area of Baden (*above*) or from Dr. Neil McCallum's Dry River in Martinbourgh is like hitting warp nine in the starship *Enterprise* after trundling along in first gear in a bashed up old Ford Escort. So, try a luxurious Pinot Gris, but remember, you need to hang on for all you're worth when one of the most intense blasts of wine flavour on Planet Wine hits you.

The astonishing truth about Pinot Blanc (*see* pages 138–9) and Pinot Gris is that they are genetically almost identical to one another – that is, damn near identical twins of the red Pinot Noir (*see* pages 84–93). Perhaps only a single gene separates this trio: so far scientists have not found it. Yet almost certainly Pinot Noir is the original version, with Blanc and Gris being natural mutations, for Pinot Noir loves to mutate. Of course, this means these grapes all share the same parents: Pinot Meunier and Gewürztraminer.

This trio of women, Collete Faller and her daughters Laurence and Catherine of Domaine Weinbach, like the Amazons of Alsatian Pinot Gris, aren't afraid of either high natural alcohol or a touch of sweetness in their Pinot Gris, for they know from long experience that these wines need the latter in order to harmonize the former. Once that happens, the honey flows, and with it comes a wild assortment of spices and pheromones. The only way you can top this experience is to add a plateful of Thai red curry.

Seyval Blanc

Welcome to the
sparkling white riot

There's an exciting story behind many of the best grapes on Planet Wine, but Seyval Blanc is simply the product of crossing Seibel 5656 with Seibel 4986. End of story.

Just like writers, artists, and musicians, some grapes need to become exiles to find themselves and astonish the world. There is no more extreme case of that destiny than Seyval Blanc. An "inferior" hybrid, the only product of its misspent youth was vast quantities of cheap and bland dry white wines in the Loire Valley before it got thrown out of there for bad behaviour. However, in the even cooler and yet more maritime climate of southern England, particularly when grown on chalk hills, like these belonging to the South Downs in East Sussex, Seyval Blanc yields wines with a unique character in which the smells of a walk on the beach mingle with pear and grapefruit aromas. Nowhere is this more striking than in the wines of Breaky Bottom, where Seyval Blanc's leading mentor, Peter Hall, makes England's best claim to wine fame. It is not the primeval-tasting, dry "Seyval Blanc" that makes up the majority of his production, but the sparkling "Cuvée Rémy Alexandre", which is far superior to any number of overpriced Champagnes. Yes, there's some gold foil on the neck of the bottle but, what's important is not anything stuck on the outside of the bottle, it's the white riot *inside*.

Tempranillo
Tinta Roriz
Aragonês

Tempranillo is one of only a handful of red grapes to have shot from almost complete oblivion to global fame in recent times. A generation ago it was regarded as just one of the grapes from which Spanish classics such as Rioja and the much more expensive Vega Sicilia were made. Now the red grape with the black-olive aroma is a red-hot item, and while commercial production has not yet gone global, it is being planted experimentally in warmer wine-growing regions at all points on the compass. One man, Alejandro Fernández, of Pesquera in Spain's Ribera del Duero region, set this revolution going during the 1980s by insisting on 100 per cent Tempranillo and pursuing the perfection of a luscious, smoky style that makes his red wines the equivalent of polished hard rock. Since then, he has gone on to found a second Ribera del Duero estate called Condado de Haza; another just outside the Toro region called Dehesa la Granja, and yet another in the La Mancha region called El Vínculo. All four stages of Fernandez's mighty red wine rocket are fuelled by 100 per cent Tempranillo! Over the border from Spain in Portugal, Tempranillo is known as Roriz or Aragonês and has recently begun making headlines here, too. Aragonês enabled João Portugal Ramos's (*left*) "Marqués de Borba Reserva" from Alentejo to become a sensation with the first vintage, 1997. And no wonder. Behind the echoing thunder and black heat of the berry is a tantalizing delicacy that demands "Again!"

Tempranillo used to be lost in the Iberian woods, its rich-berry flavour boxed in by the overpowering smell of vanilla from the barrels of American oak where it spent its youth and middle age. Now the winemakers of Spain and Portugal have set it free and we can experience the attraction of its youthful charms.

Rocketing out of the woods

Teroldego

In northeastern Italy, Elizabetta Foradori of Trentino is a one-woman movement; 400 years ago she would probably have been burnt at the stake. Her work has nothing to do with black magic, but everything to do with vine nurturing. It is an unrelenting search for ways to achieve equal rights for the Teroldego grape, aligning it with the most-esteemed, Italian red wine grapes, Sangiovese and Nebbiolo.

One woman wonder

When Foradori began her work, Teroldego was almost extinct as a quality grape, because the vine material available had been ruthlessly selected for the mass production of red plonk; most Teroldego wines tasted thin, tart, and bitter. Her revolution involved reversing this process and rigorously selecting clonal material based on ripe, fruit flavours and robust vine health. The result is red wines which are dark and energetic, with a mountain freshness from the rock faces that almost surround the Campo Rotaliano plain where they grow. Foradori calls her "basic" red "Foradori", and the wine that is Teroldego's claim to greatness "Granato".

Lagrein

It was only during the mid 1990s that a dozen or so Lagrein producers rescued the grape from the "Dark Side". Through better vineyard practices, together with more care in the cellar, they managed to tame the wild, mountain man of Italian Alpine grapes. Not that this process has robbed the wine of its primal energy or bear-like stature, as wines such as the *riserva* from Abtei Muri-Gries prove. The astonishing thing is that not only have Lagrein wines become less monolithically dark, but that they have also proved ever more diverse in aroma and style. At the elegant end of the spectrum are the sleek yet intensely fragrant wines from Franz Haas, which are almost transparent in their allegiance to the "Light Side" of the red wine "Force". The only darkness here is in the soul of their maker, who drives himself and his wines along in a relentless struggle to achieve vinous nirvana in a region whose traditional focus is centred around quaffing wines for skiers and hikers.

Lagrein used to be called Lagrein Dunkel: "Lagrein the Dark". It might have become the Goth of Italy's Alto Adige: worshipped for its unrelenting hardness by wine punks, but lost to anyone interested in fruity aromas and harmonious, ripe flavours.

Beware the dark side of the grape!

Tourigia Nacional et al

Return of the natives

A new mega-star was born of the Portuguese red wine boom of the 1990s, and its name was Touriga Nacional. That sounds like Iberian speed metal, and on the steep, granitic slopes of the mighty Douro Valley, in northern Portugal, this grape can indeed yield wines that pack a mighty punch of metallic-tasting, dry tannin, alcohol, and the blackest of berry flavours. No wonder they've become a cult. In the mad rush to jump on the Touriga Nacional bandwagon, the plethora of other grapes indigenous to the Douro have been too often forgotten by local winemakers, or dismissed as mere backing singers – that is "blending material" for the superstar grape.

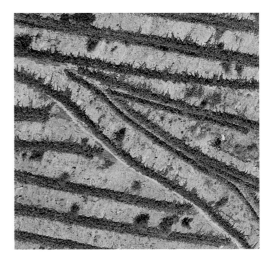

Dirk van der Niepoort of the Niepoort port company believes in the power of genetic diversity to craft compelling red wine flavours in Portugal's Douro Valley. He has been developing a range of new Douro red and white wines from two handfuls of half-forgotten and completely forgotten native grapes for more than a decade. In fact, for the wine beat poet of Portuguese winemaking, the other indigenous grapes of the Douro are far more interesting than Touriga Nacional.

Drink Van der Niepoort's red "Redoma Tinto", a complex blend dominated by the Tinta Amarela, Touriga Francesca, and Roriz grapes (*see* page 144). Touriga Nacional is no more than a pinch of spice in this staggeringly complex brew. His dry white "Redoma Branca" is even more revolutionary, relying on grapes from ancient vines of varieties like Rabigato, Codega, and Viosinho, that are seldom planted anymore. The actual vines responsible for this wine, in which freshness and power are exactly matched, are no less ancient than the grape varieties. Niepoort's daring mix of wine archaeology and futuristic vision defy all the contemporary categories and easy descriptors. All my adjectives seem spent when faced with the embryonic offspring of the future and the past in my glass! But I know that I must drink this mystery to grasp it…

Viognier

Sky-high alcoholic strength and down-in-the-dumps acidity make many of the wines from this ultra-fashionable grape of the 1990s as ponderously dull and leadenly lumpen as dry white wine gets. Their message is that somebody should have thought harder about whether this was the right place to plant this fickle grape before it was too late. Many wine critics make a big fuss about this grape, though you never see them drinking its wines unless someone else is paying. Even its presence in its home region, Condrieu in the Rhône valley a short drive south of Lyon, looks more like an accident of history than a marriage made in heaven. I might have given up on it completely if it were not for a few magical moments when Viognier utterly seduced me.

When this diva is on top of the world, then Viognier is one of *the* most seductive dry white wines – full stop. All the bombast is replaced by the aromas of summer flowers and ripe peaches; the texture is soft and caressing, with just enough acidity to taste fresh. These are not wines to bury in a dark hole in the ground in the hope that delayed satisfaction will result in an even bigger thrill, as is the case with top, dry white wines such as Riesling (*see* pages 74–83) or Chardonnay (*see* pages 56–67). No. Luscious Viogniers, like those from California wine's Mr Chainsaw Massacre, Josh Jensen (*above*) of Calera are for grabbing when the going's good.

Just who does she think she is?

Viognier is a diva grape and its moodiness has been known to put Maria Callas in the shade. In a petulant mood, it yields dry white wines with a bouquet like cheap perfume and a taste like Palmolive dissolved in vodka.

Welschriesling

Welschriesling is a Cinderella grape. With their green-apple aroma, tartness, and spritz, dry Welschrieslings are fine on a hot summer day, but they are definitely commoners. However, picked "after midnight", when many other grapes have turned to mush, Welschriesling turns into a dessert wine princess in glass stilettos with a natural wasp waist.

Mr K's midas touch

These bunches of grapes (*left*) look like nothing more than a handful of rotten raisins – or have they caught the Black Death? Yes and no. Many of the world's most sought-after dessert wines are made from grapes exactly like these Welschriesling in Alois Kracher's vineyards, close to the town of Illmitz in the Burgenland region of Austria. Here, on the banks of the Neusiedler See – in spite of the reed beds and exceptional bird life, the lake reaches a depth of only two metres (around six feet) – conditions are ideal for the development of *Botrytis cinerea*, better known as "noble rot". This fungus is actually only "noble" when it strikes fully ripe grapes during the weeks immediately prior to harvest (on unique grapes it is just "rot" rot). When the affected bunches then shrivel in the autumn sunshine, they are harvested and pressed separately – and lo! A golden wine of exquisite lasciviousness. No wonder Kracher himself prefers this honeyed elixir in the kind of quantity he's shown holding, rather than in the half-bottles in which he normally sells it. That's seldom a problem here, though. Unlike most other places famous for dessert wine production, it is possible to produce them in quantity just about every year.

Zinfandel
Primitivo

Zin always has plenty of alcohol, seldom tasting good with fewer than 14 degrees of the stuff, particularly when produced from century-old vineyards in its Californian "homeland", Sonoma County, by top-gun producers such as Brogan, Mantinelli, Ridge, and Scherrer. Fred Scherrer (*left*) is the leader of the latest generation of Sonoma County Zin-pioneers, making some of the most hedonistic, gonzo wines on Planet Wine from this grape. Let the good times roll!

The search for Zinfandel's roots was probably the longest and most convoluted piece of detective work in the history of grape geneology. On paper, it made its way from the royal Austro-Hungarian nurseries in Vienna to the East Coast of America during the 1820s, and from there to California immediately after the gold rush of 1849. By the late 1980s, vine scientists had recognized the extreme similarities between Zinfandel and the Primitivo grape of Apulia, at Italy's heel. Were the two in fact different clones of the same variety? This now appears to be the case, although a third element was recently added to the puzzle when DNA analysis revealed the rare Croatian Crljenak Kastelanski grape to be the same variety. Vine scientists now refer to the grape as ZPC, and conjecture that it made its way to California via Vienna and to Apulia from Croatia. But has this solved the mystery of the origins of this ultimate original once and for all? Watch this space…

Zinfandel is the original "original" grape. The one that blazed the trail of the global movement back to regional wine specialties long before anyone was talking about globalization. Not only are the opulent raspberry and spice flavours of Zin the object of one of the most fanatical red wine cults on the planet ("Life is Hell without Zinfandel" and "I've got a head made for business and a body made for Zin" are just two of its many slogans), but it is the grape that taught wine to rock. Without my consumption of a gigantic quantity of this drug over two decades, I would never have been able to sex-up this report on Planet Wine, as I have so shamelessly done. I freely admit that I was and am frequently high on Zin. This is a similar kind of intoxication you get from cannabis or from riding a fast motorcycle. Drinking the Harley-Davidson of wines was always inspiring, though, even if I often felt "Zinned out" afterwards.

Index of Estates and Producers

Index

Picture Credits

Mitchell Beazley would like to thank the following for their kind permission to reproduce the photographs in this book.

Key t top b bottom l left r right

Endpapers Amin Khadr; 6–7 Octopus Publishing Group/Russell Sadur; 8 Root Stock/Hendrik Holler; 9 Science Photo Library/Andrew Syred; 10 De Trafford Wines/Aidan Morton; 11 Root Stock/Hendrik Holler; 12 Patrick Eagar; 13 Amin Khadr; 14 Scope/Jean Luc Barde; 15 t & b VinVinoLife; 16 Science Photo Library/Microfield Scientific Ltd; 17 Scope/Jacques Guillard; 18 Domaine Clarence Dillon/Photographed by Burdin/Private Collection; 19 Piper-Heidsieck; 20 b Max/PPP; 20–21 t Amin Khadr; 22–23 Jacob's Creek/Pernod Ricard; 24–25 VinVinoLife; 26–27 t & b Root Stock/Hendrik Holler; 28 Rustenberg Winery; 29 Viader Vineyard/Cathy Bolduc; 30 t Wowe; 30 b & 31 Ridge Vineyards; 32 t & b Niebaum-Coppola/Gundolf Pfotenhauer; 33 Stag's Leap Wine Cellar/Robin White; 34 Tertre–Rôteboeuf; 35 Octopus Publishing Group/Jason Lowe; 36 b Root Stock/Hendrik Holler; 36–37 t Patrick Eagar; 37 b Wowe; 38 Laboratoire de Michel Rolland; 39 Root Stock/Hendrik Holler; 40–41 Rockford Wines; 43 Adrian Lander/Stokyard; 44 Courtesy of Mount Langi Ghiran; 45 Ursula Heinzelmann; 46 Root Stock/Hendrik Holler; 47 Steven Morris; 48 & 49 Wowe; 50–51 Amin Khadr; 52 VinVinoLife; 53 Claes Löfgren/winepictures.com; 54 t Scope/Jean Luc Barde; 54 b Guido Jansegers/Château Mansenoble; 55 Claes Löfgren/winepictures.com; 56 Leeuwin Estate; 57 Domaine des Comtes Lafon/Morris & Verdin; 58 Root Stock/Hendrik Holler; 59 Claes Löfgren/winepictures.com; 60–61 Scope/Sara Matthews; 62–63 Root Stock/Hendrik Holler; 64 Network/Michael Amendolia; 65 Roland Velich/Manfred Klimek; 66 Hubert Laferrere/Domaine Saint Denis; 67 t Root Stock/Hendrik Holler; 67 b Claes Löfgren/winepictures.com; 68 t St Michael–Eppan; 68 b www.ulrikeholsten.de; 69 Wowe; 70–71 t Faber & Partner; 71 b Manfred Tement; 72 Didier Dagueneau; 73 Claes Löfgren/winepictures.com; 74–75 Amin Khadr; 76 Southlight Photo Library/Don Brice; 77 Grosset Wines; 78 Wowe; 79 Chateau (Kastiel) Bela; 80 Claes Löfgren/winepictures.com; 81 John Thompson/Crawford River; 82 Inniskillin; 83 VinVinoLife; 84–85 Cornish Point/Suellen Boag; 86 Maison Nicholas Potel; 87 Domaine Charles Audoin; 88 Amin Khadr; 89 Claypix.com/Clay McLachlan; 90 Georg Fromm Weinbau/Ralph Feiner; 91 John Rizzo Studio/Chris Buffington; 92 Stonecutter/Roger Pemberton; 93 t www.herbertlehmann.com; 93 b Roy Metzdorf; 94 b Isole e Olena/Liberty Wine; 94–95 t Claes Löfgren/winepictures.com; 96 Castello di Ama: Michelangelo Pistaletto/Attilio Maranzano; 97 Wowe; 98 Château Julien; 99 Shafer Vineyards; 100–101 Octopus Publishing Group/Jason Lowe; 101 t Olivier Briedél/Château Lavabre; 102 Kirk Irwin/I & I Images; 103 Anja Weber/Springfontein; 104–105 Root Stock/Hendrik Holler; 106 Brian Jordan; 107 Gaia Wines; 108 & 109 Braida di Bologna Giacomo; 110 Weingut Krutzler; 111 l Paul Achs; 111 r & 112 Claes Löfgren/winepictures.com; 113 t Château Cheval Blanc/Gérard Uféras; 113 b VinVinoLife; 114 Root Stock/Hendrik Holler; 115 Janet Price; 116 Claes Löfgren/winepictures.com; 117 Mike Dubrovic; 118 Istvân Szepsy/Top Selection; 119 www.herbertlehmann.com; 120 Adrian Lander/Stok-yard; 121 www.herbertlehmann.com; 122 The Pieropan Family; 123 Cometa Planeta/Enotria Winecellars UK; 124 Wowe; 125 t Martin Foradori/J Hofstätter; 125 b DWI/Dieth; 126 Octopus Publishing Group/Jason Lowe; 127 Bonny Doon Vineyard/Alex Krause; 128 Claes Löfgren/winepictures.com; 129 Scope/Jacques Guillard; 130 Lowell Jooste at Klein Constantia Estate; 131 Harald Thüring; 132 Claes Löfgren/winepictures.com; 133 Wowe; 134 Marqués de Griñón; 135 Wowe; 136 VinVinoLife; 137 Kanonkop Winery; 138 Harald Thüring; 139 Weingut Dr Wehrheim; 140 t Ihringer Winklerberg Vineyard, Germany's warmest vineyard; 140 b Dr Neil McCallum/Dry River; 141 Domaine Weinbach; 142 & 143 Breaky Bottom Vineyard/Christina Hall; 144 & 145 Claes Löfgren/winepictures.com; 146 Henning Bornemann Mücher; 147 Wowe; 148 t Janet Price; 148 b VinVinoLife; 149 Manfred Klimek/Wine & Partners; 150 DWI/Dieth; 151 Calera Wines; 152 Weingut Weinlaubenhof Kracher/Wine & Partners; 153 Manfred Klimek/Wine & Partners; 154 Timm Eubanks; 155 t Accademia dei Racemi; 155 b Florian Bolk.

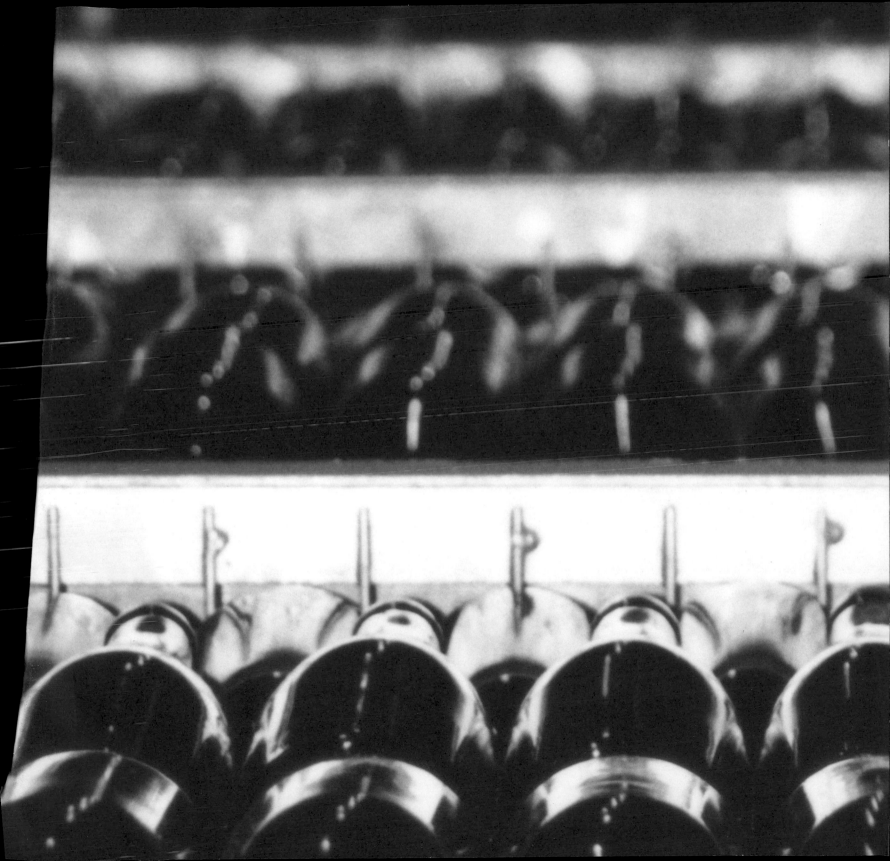